Coloring Books for Grownups

DAY OF THE DEAD CATS

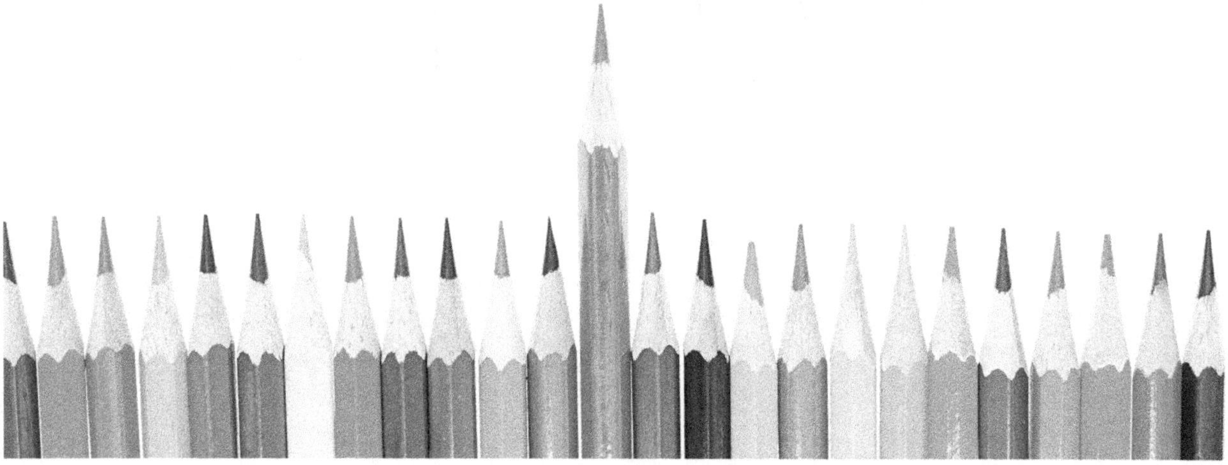

Chiquita publishing

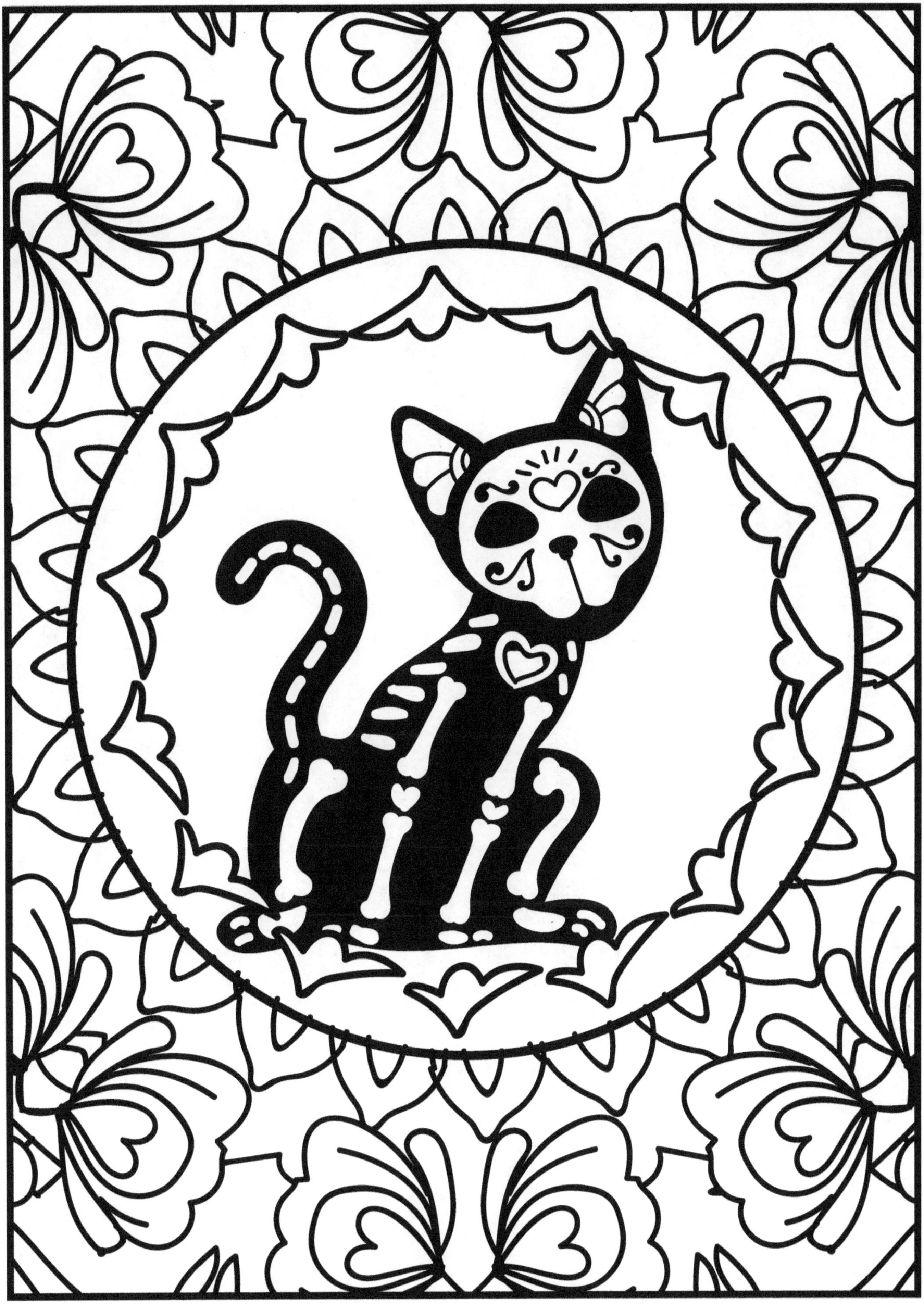

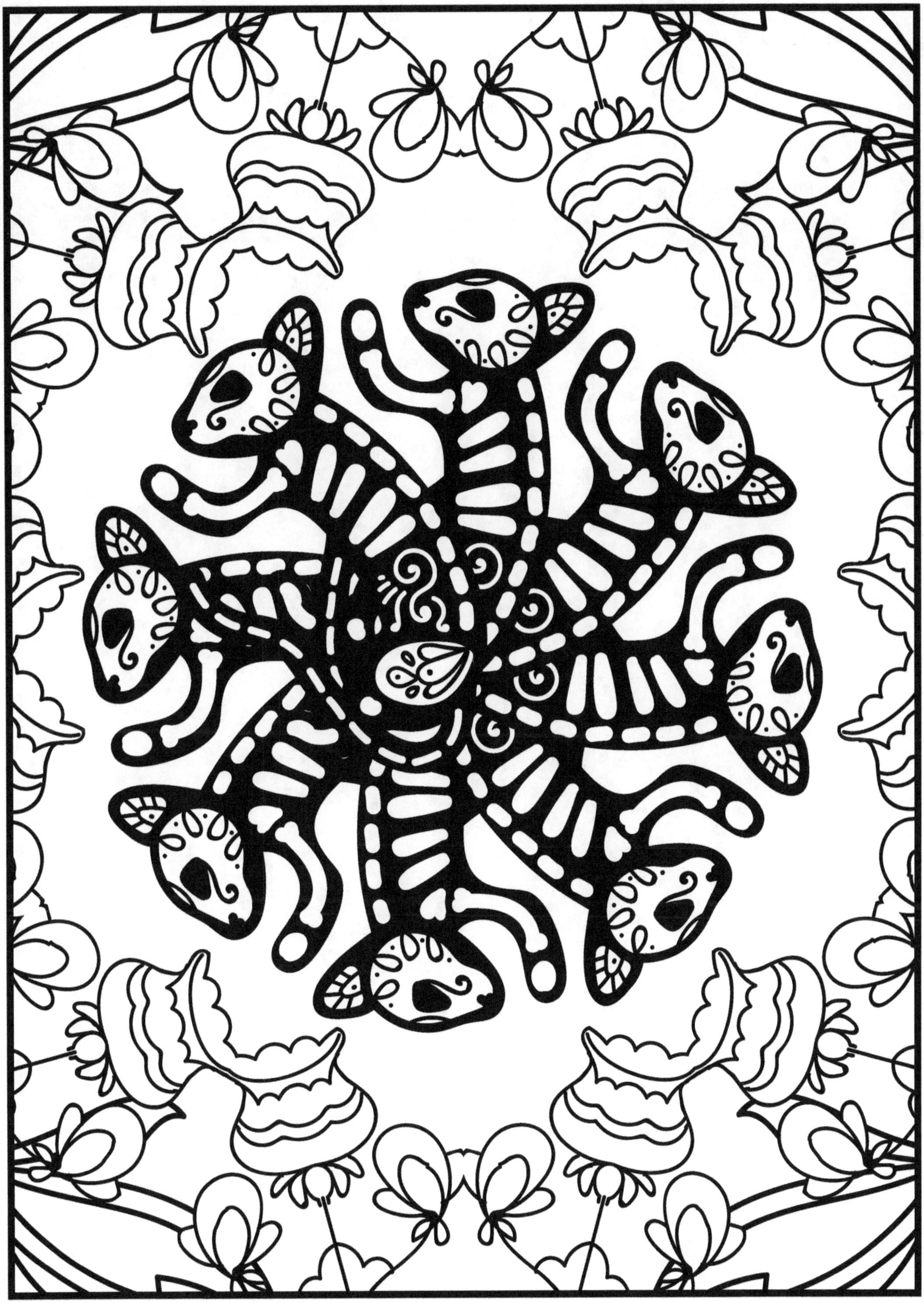

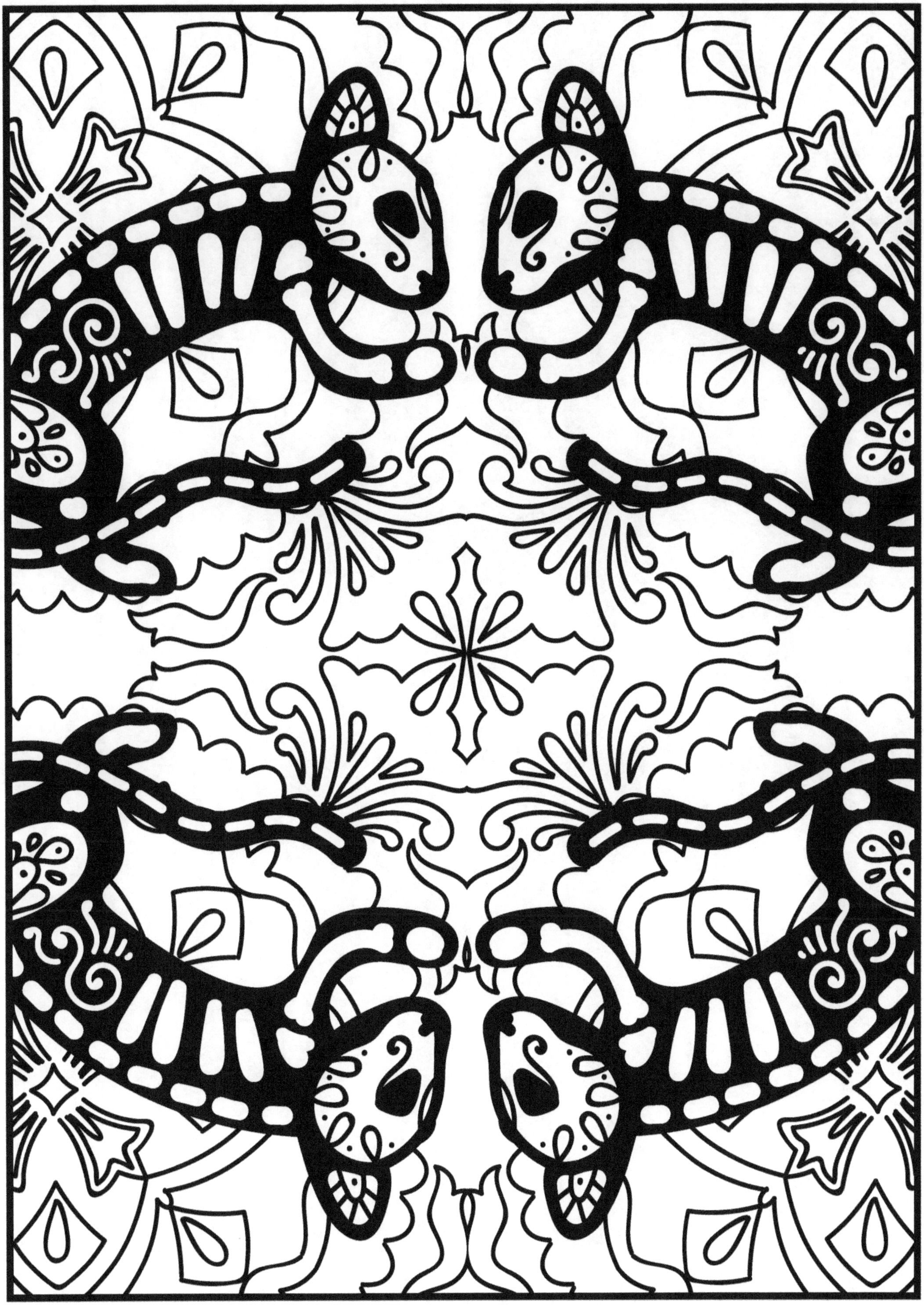

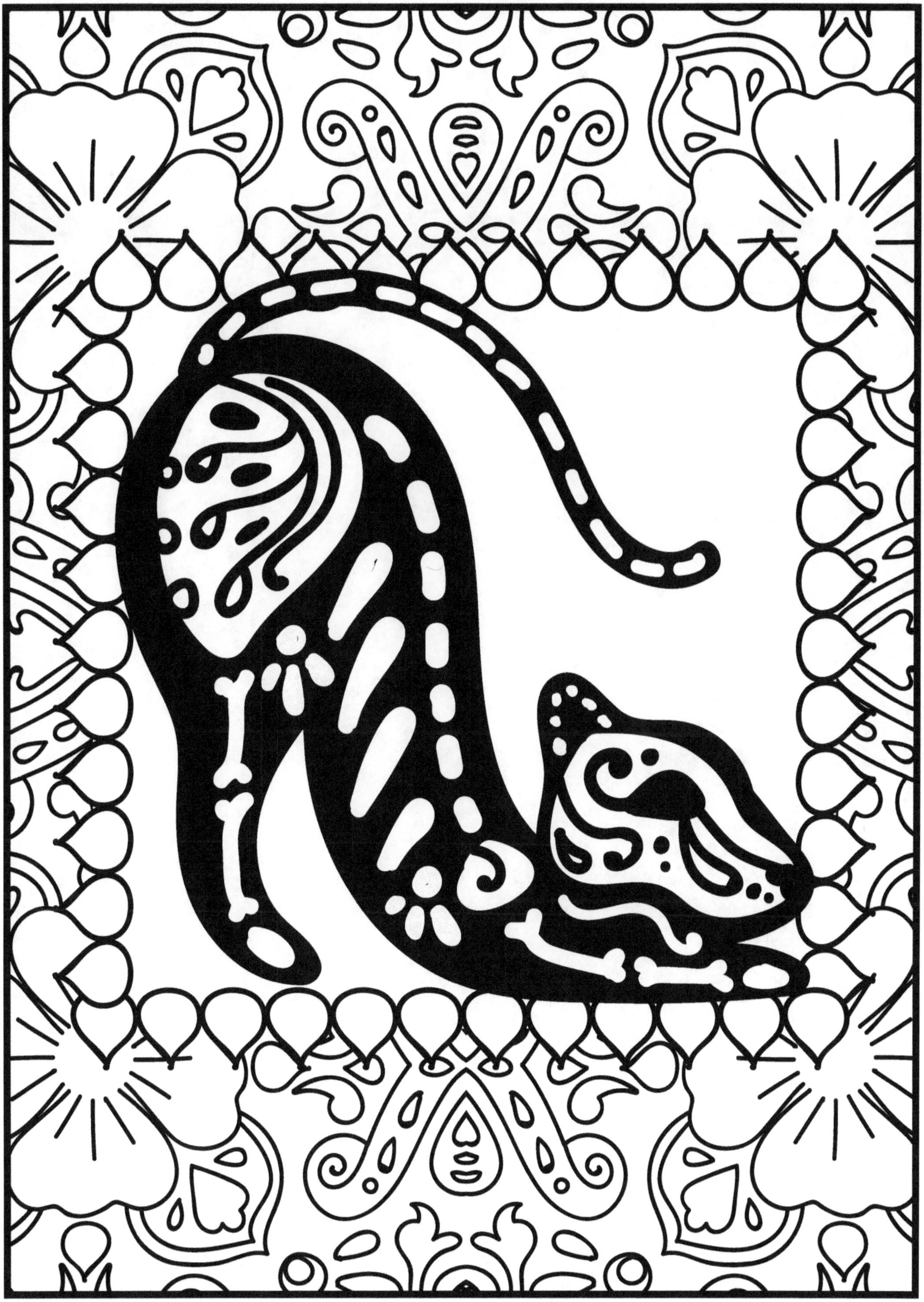

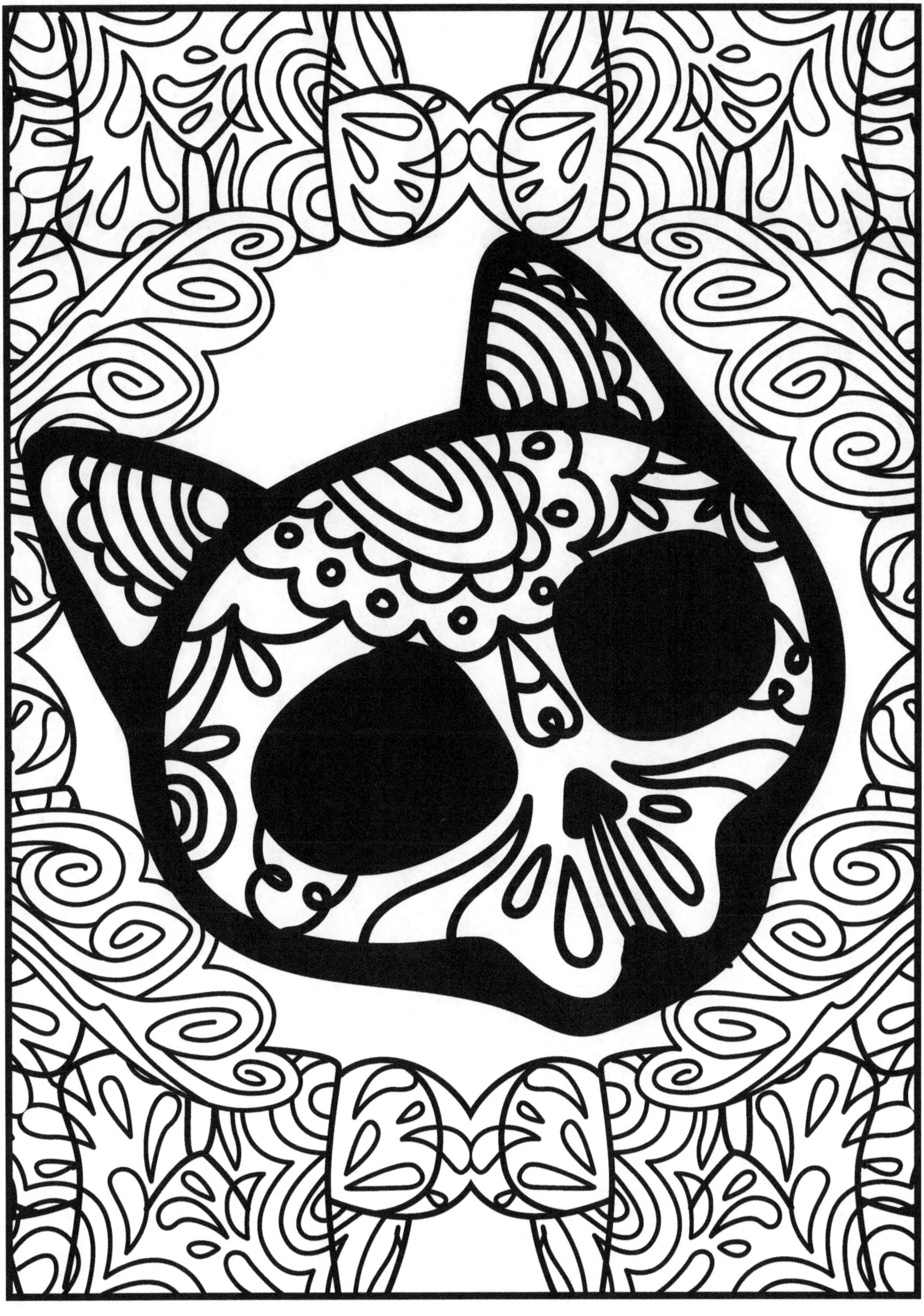

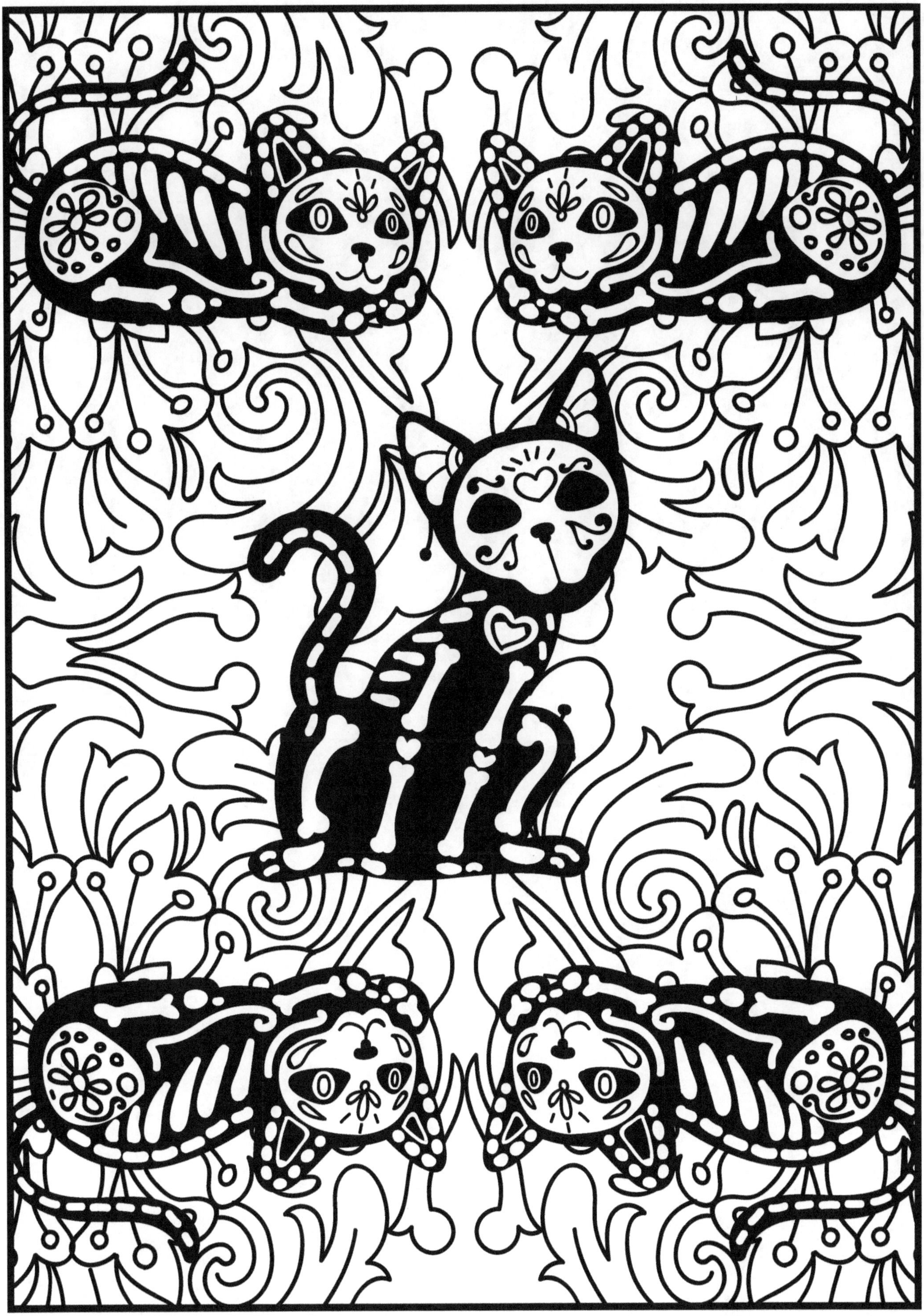

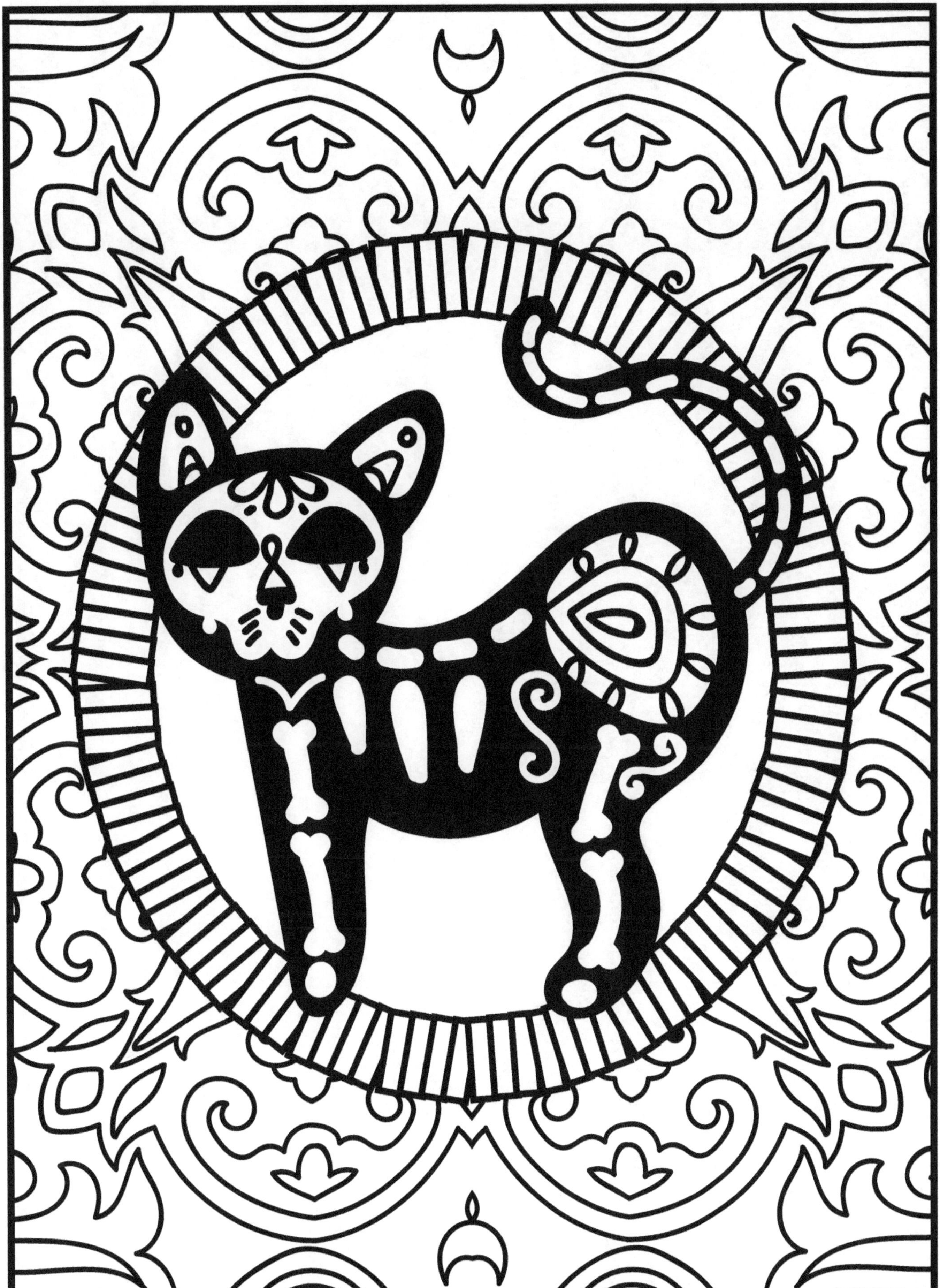

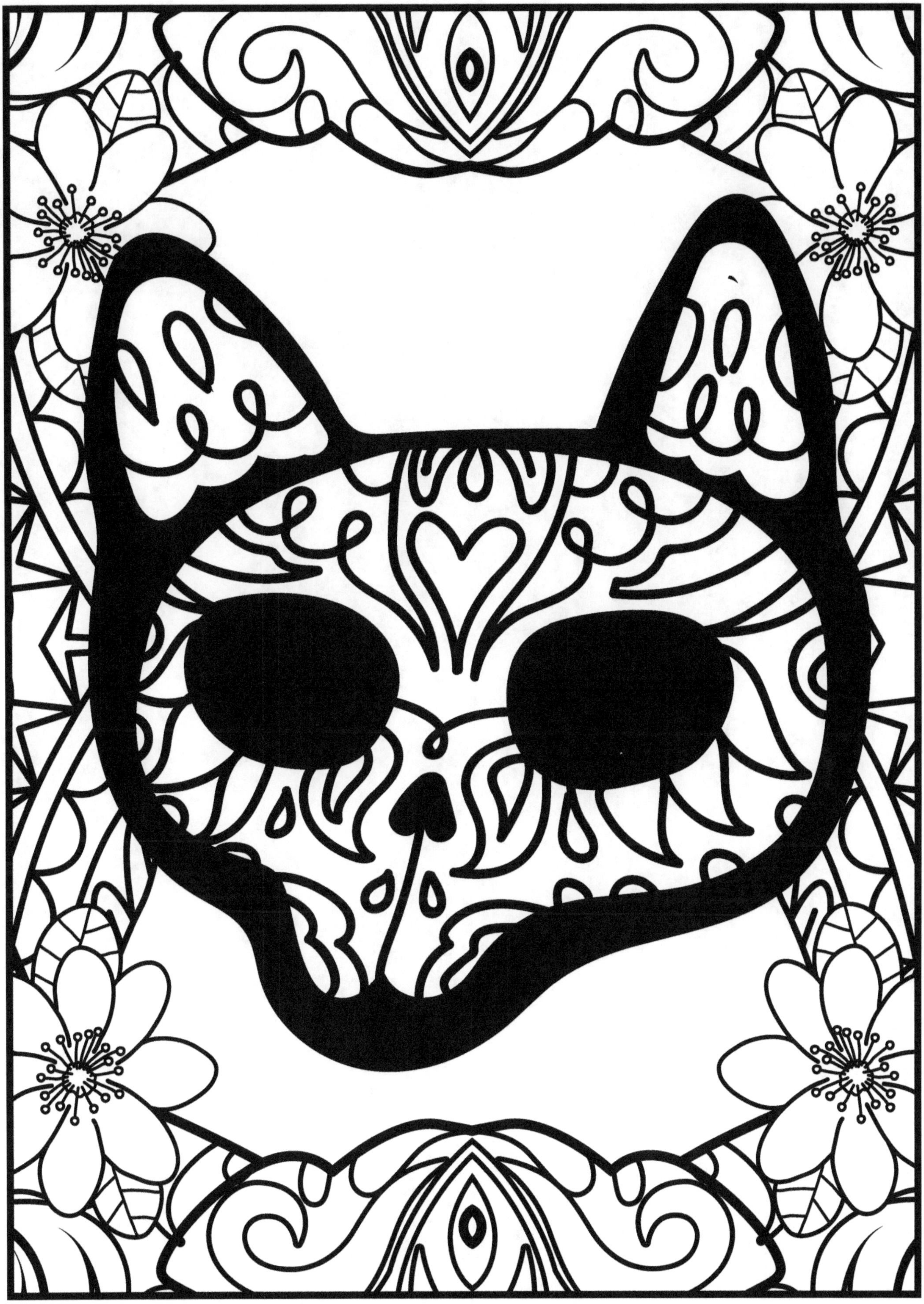

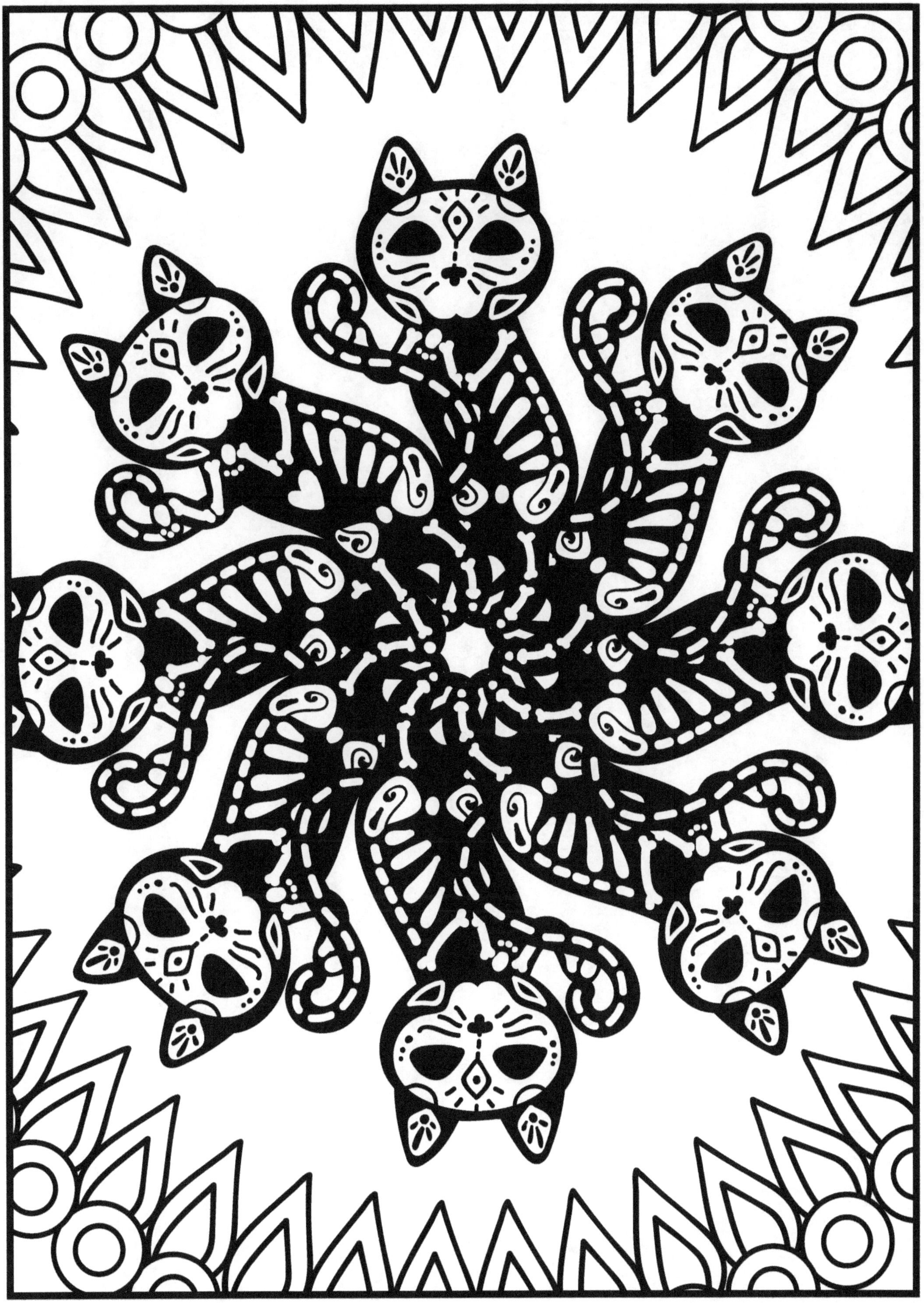

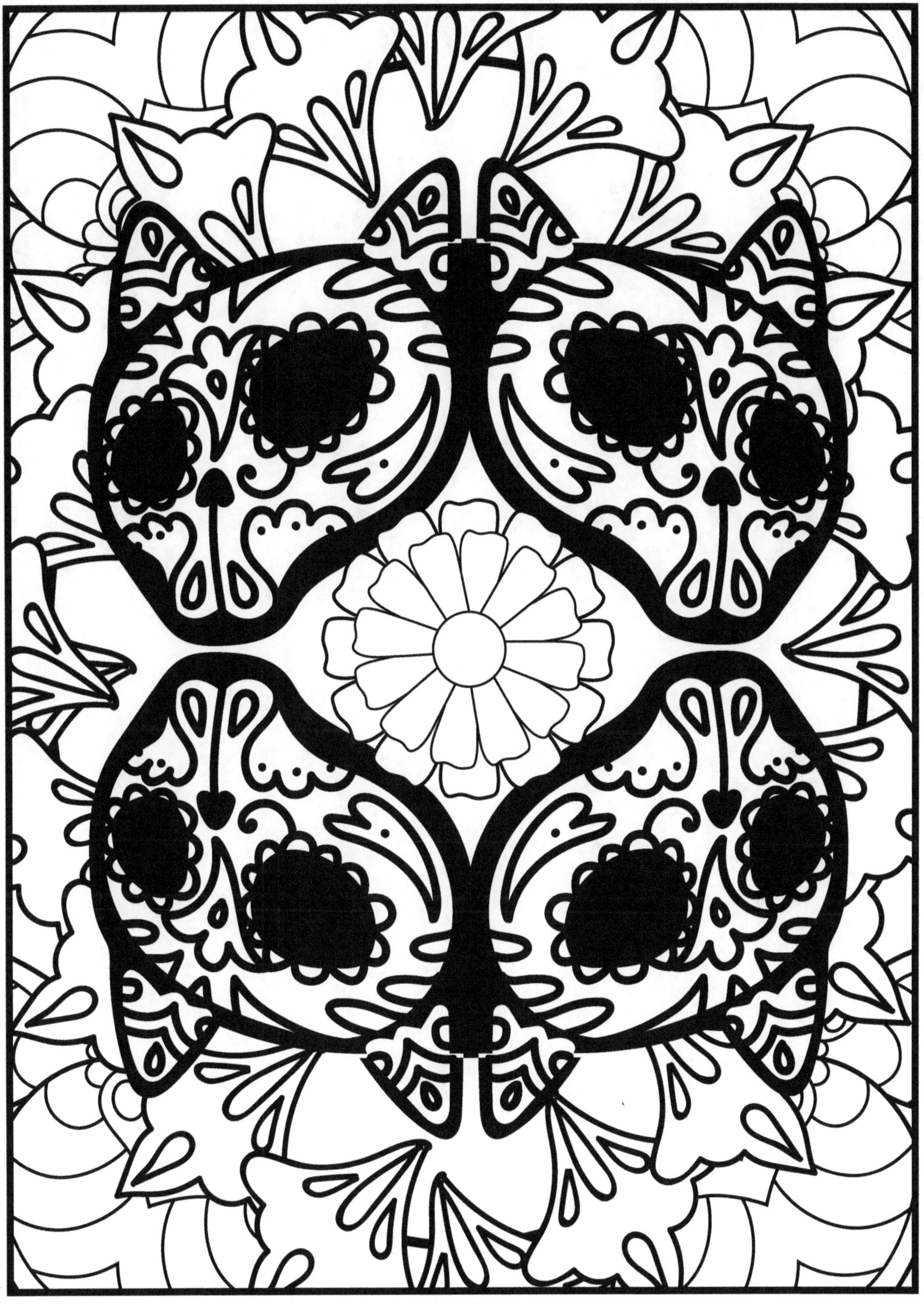

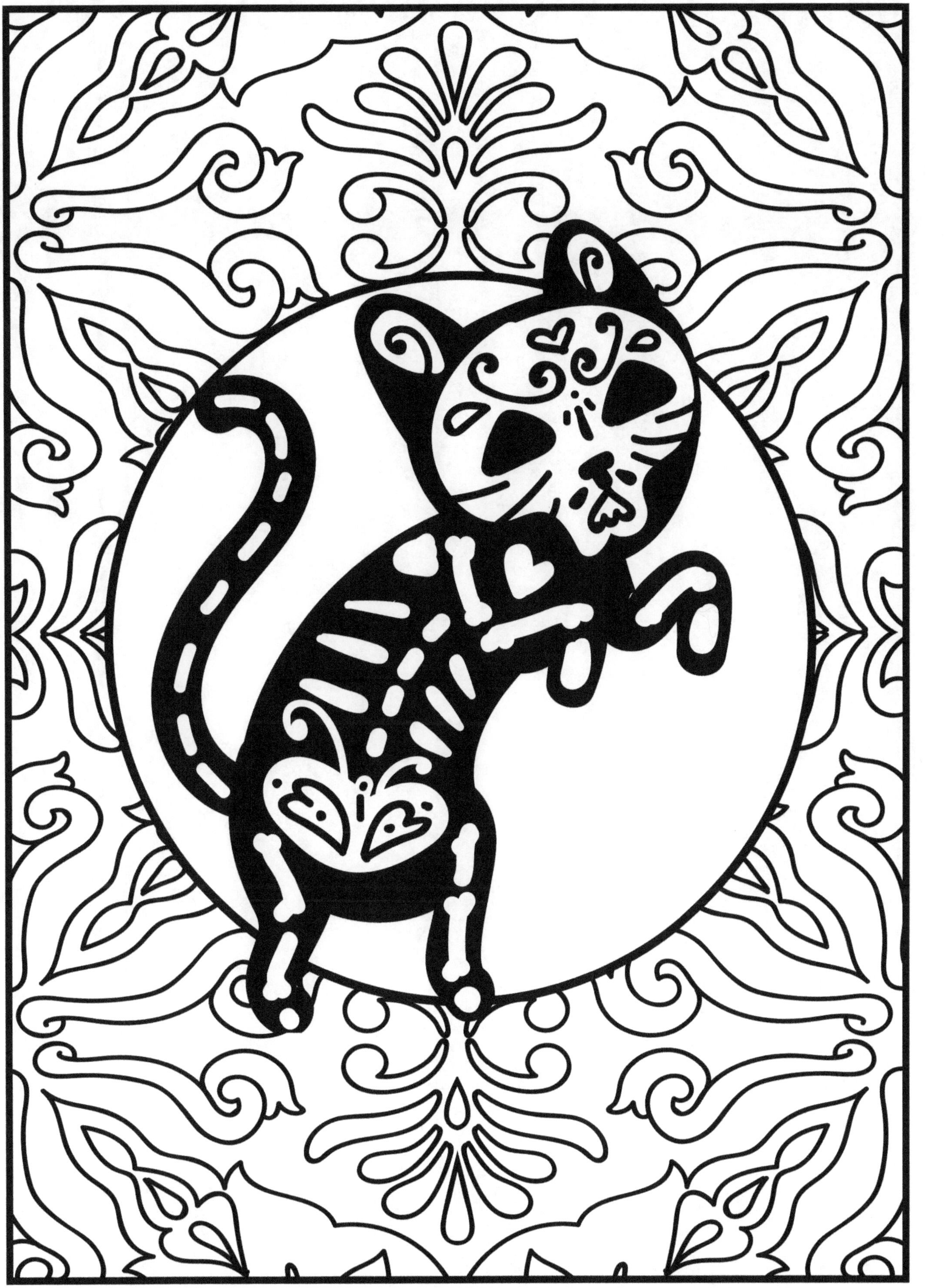

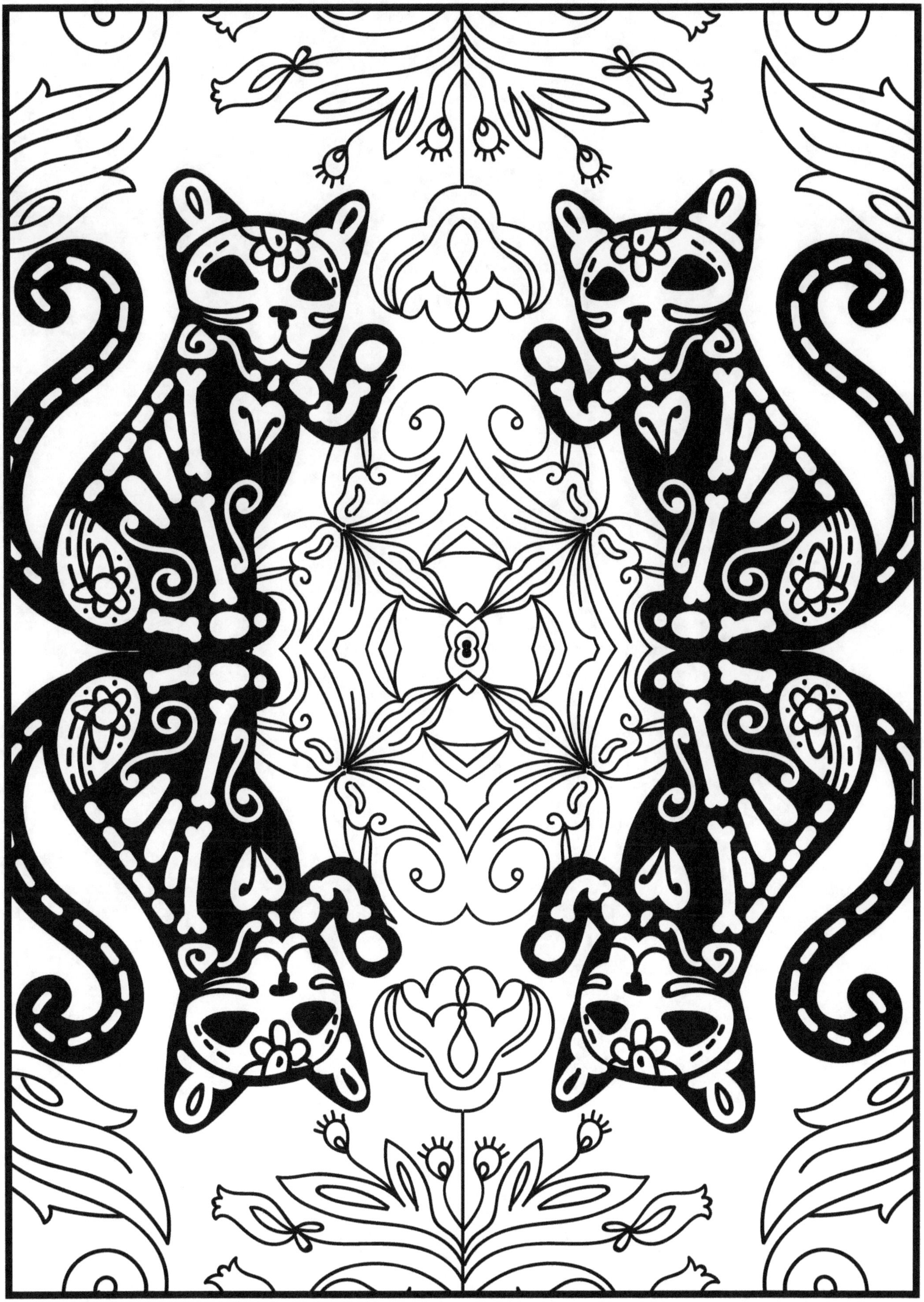

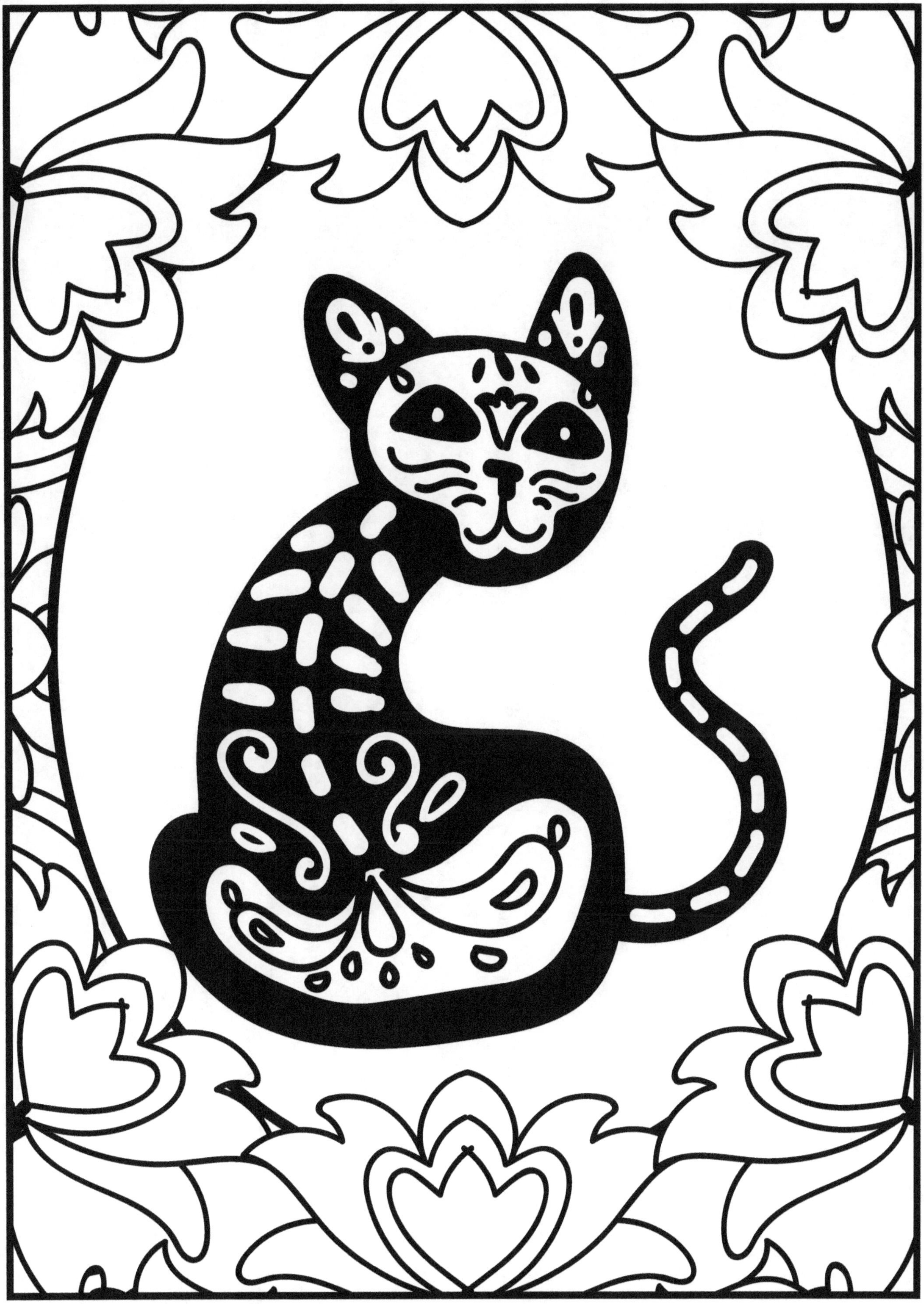

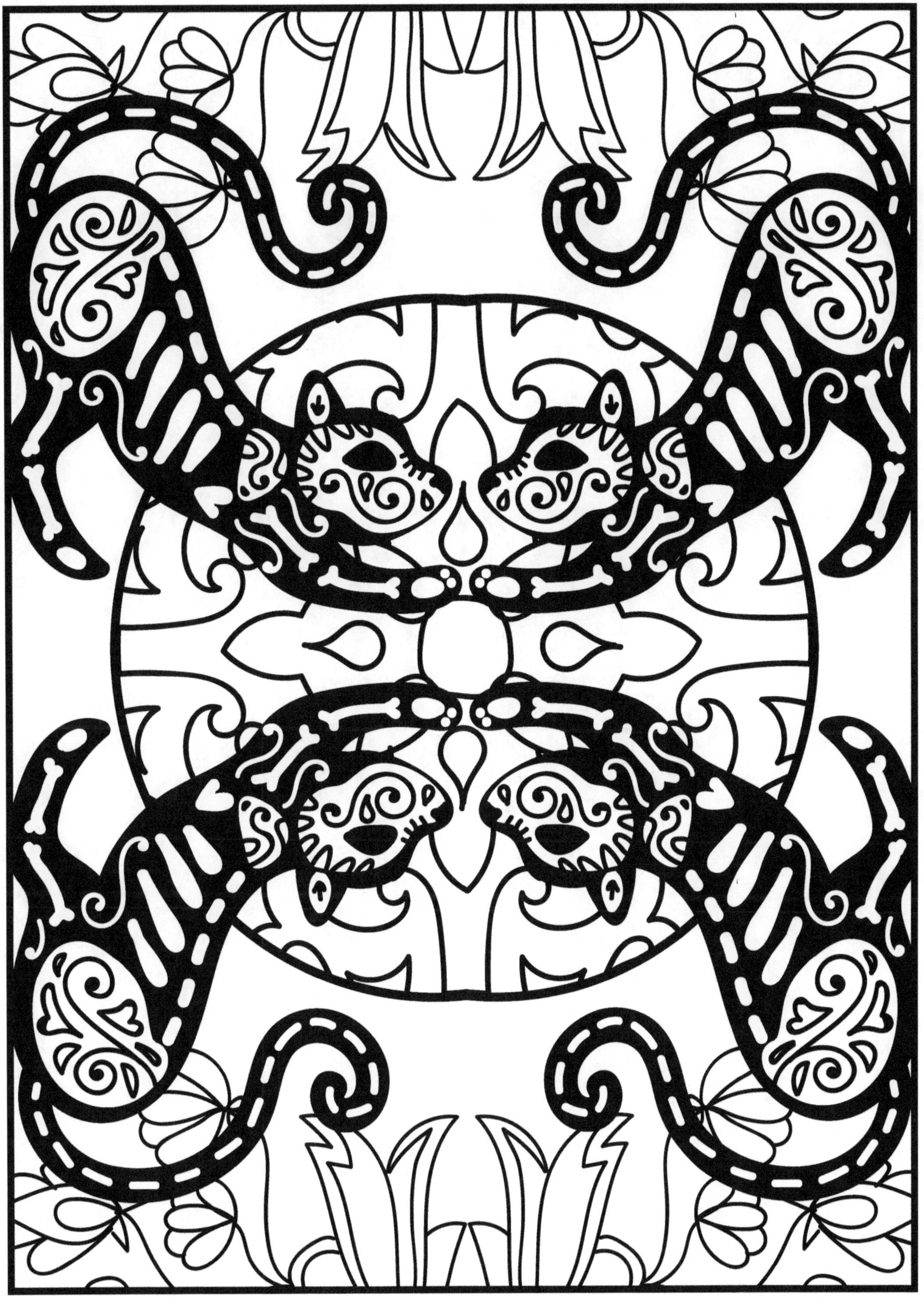

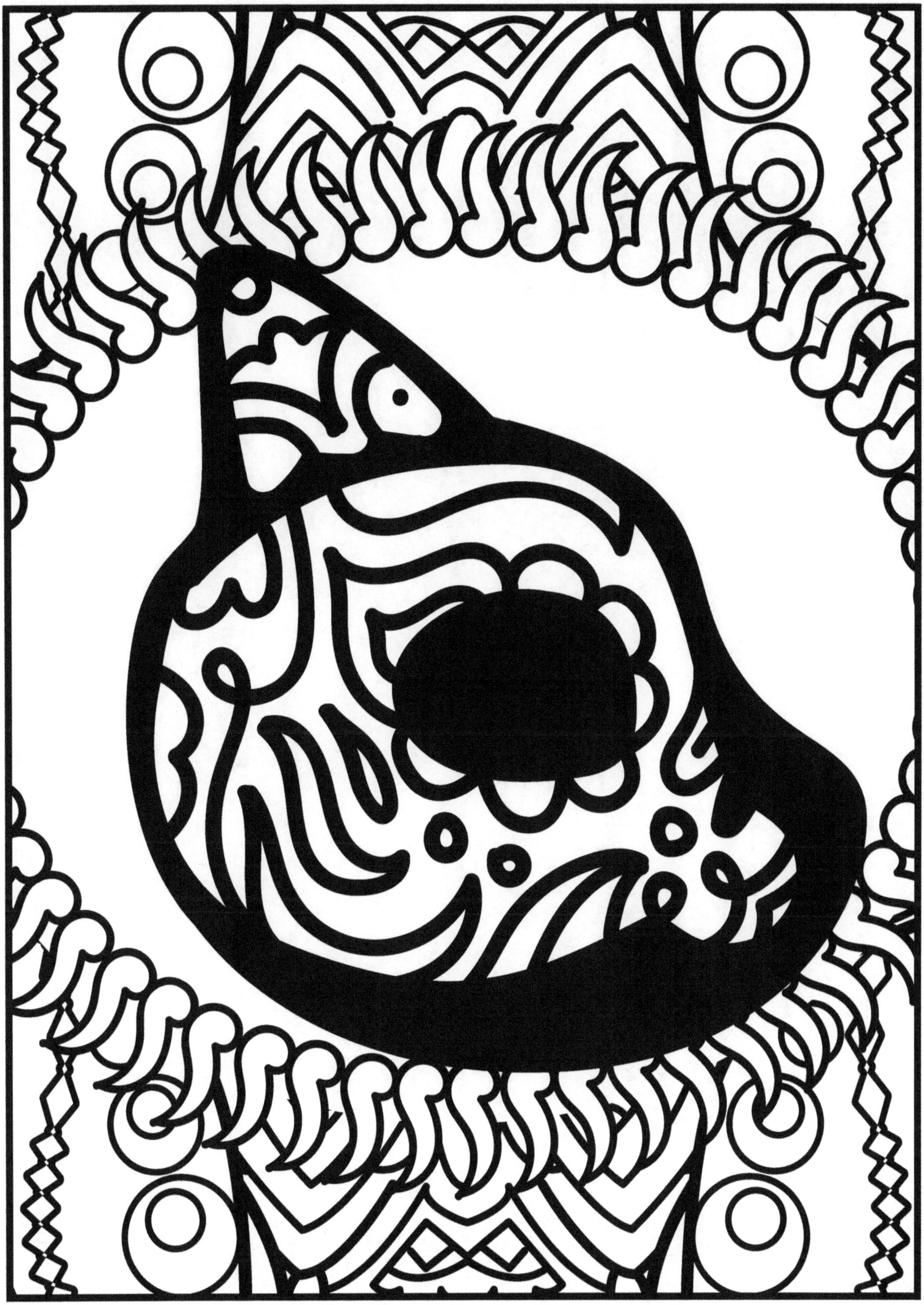

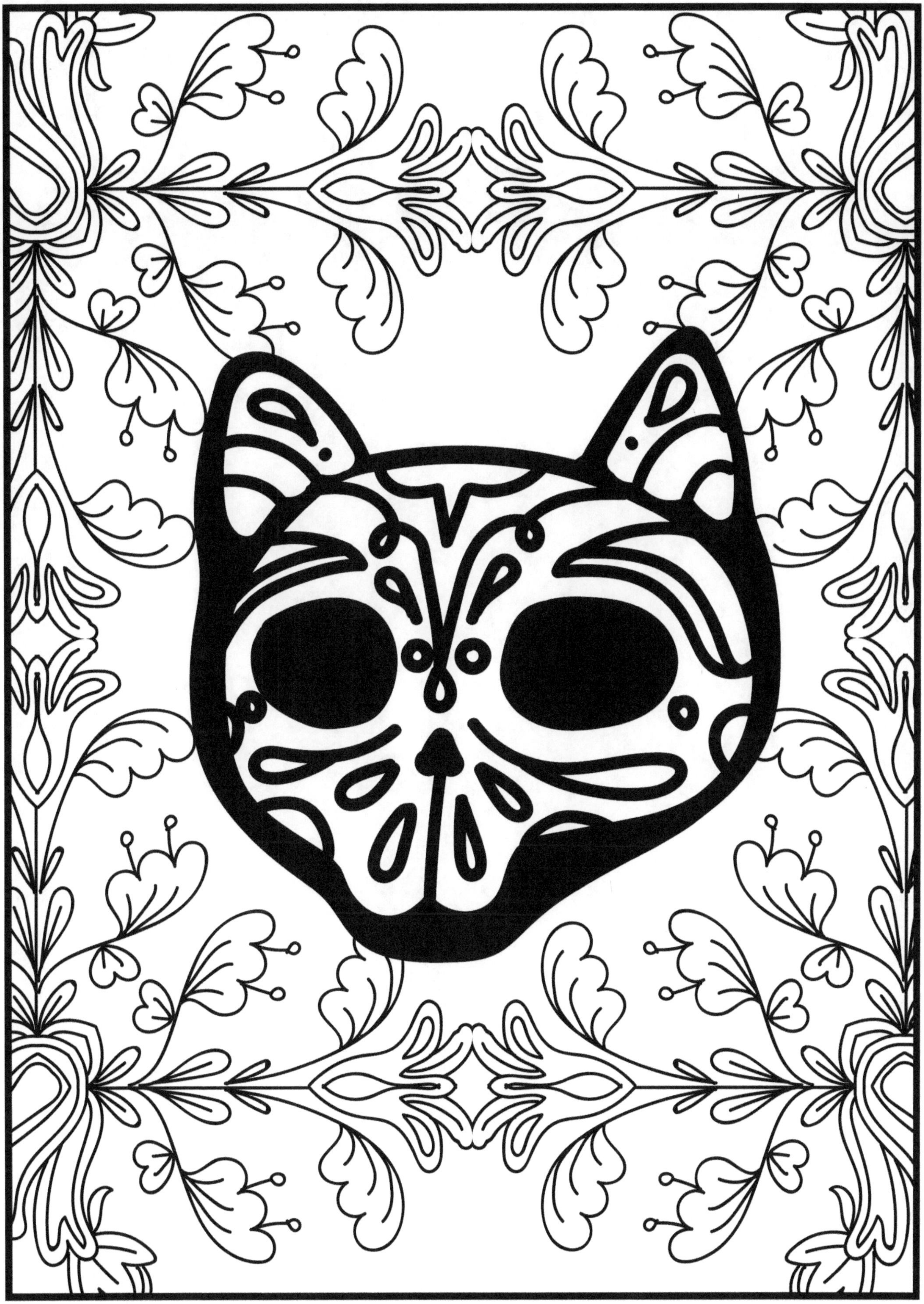

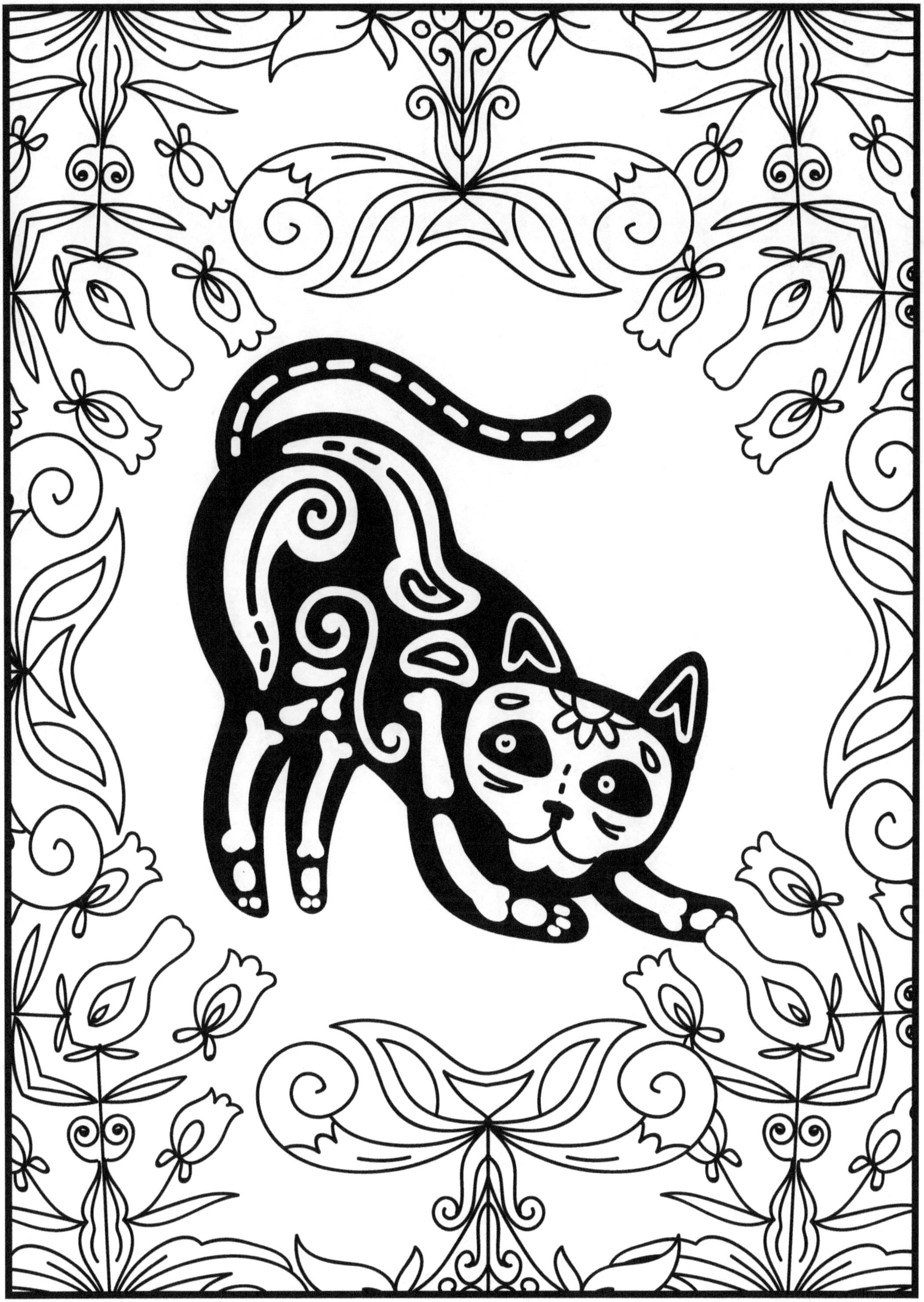

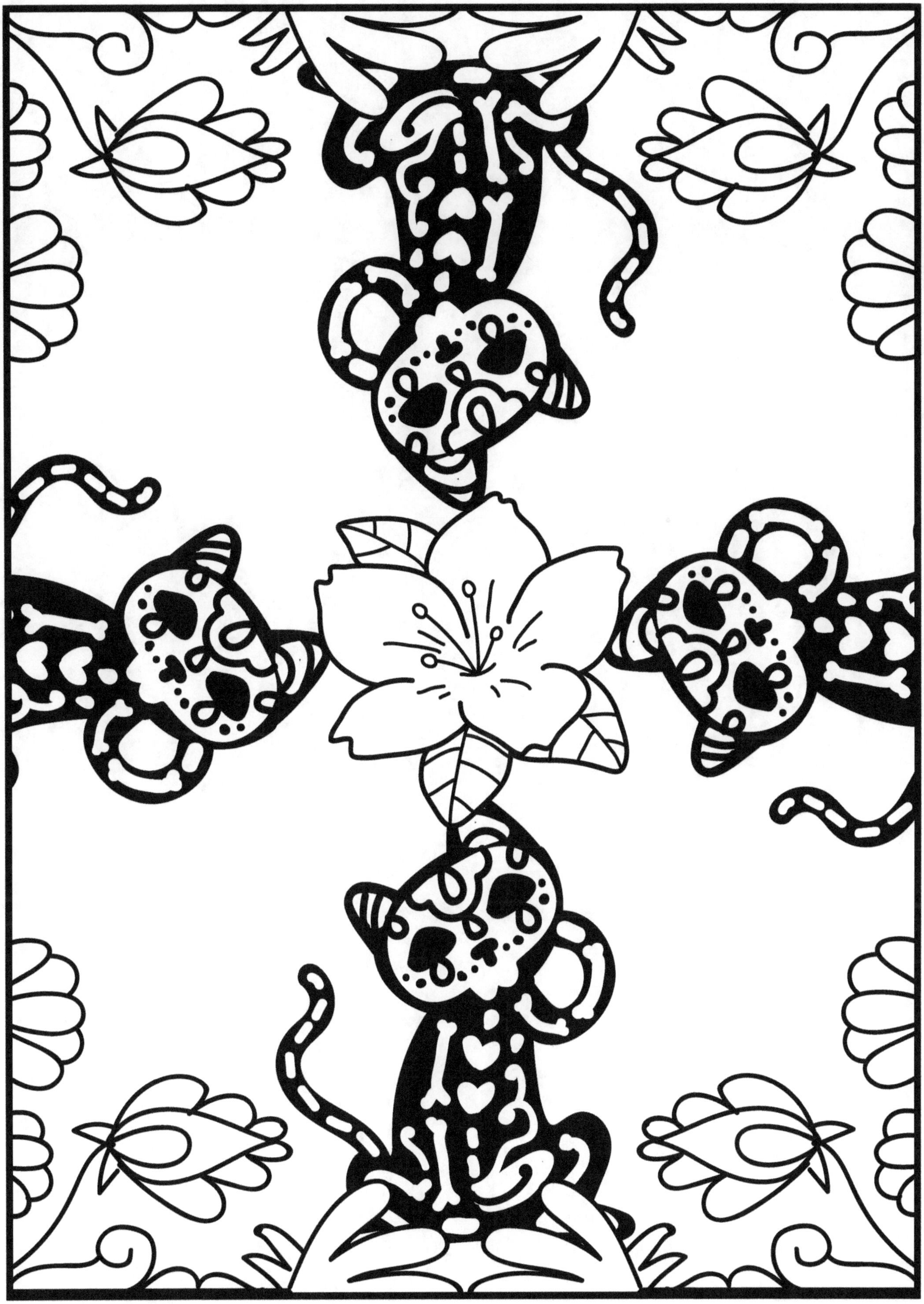

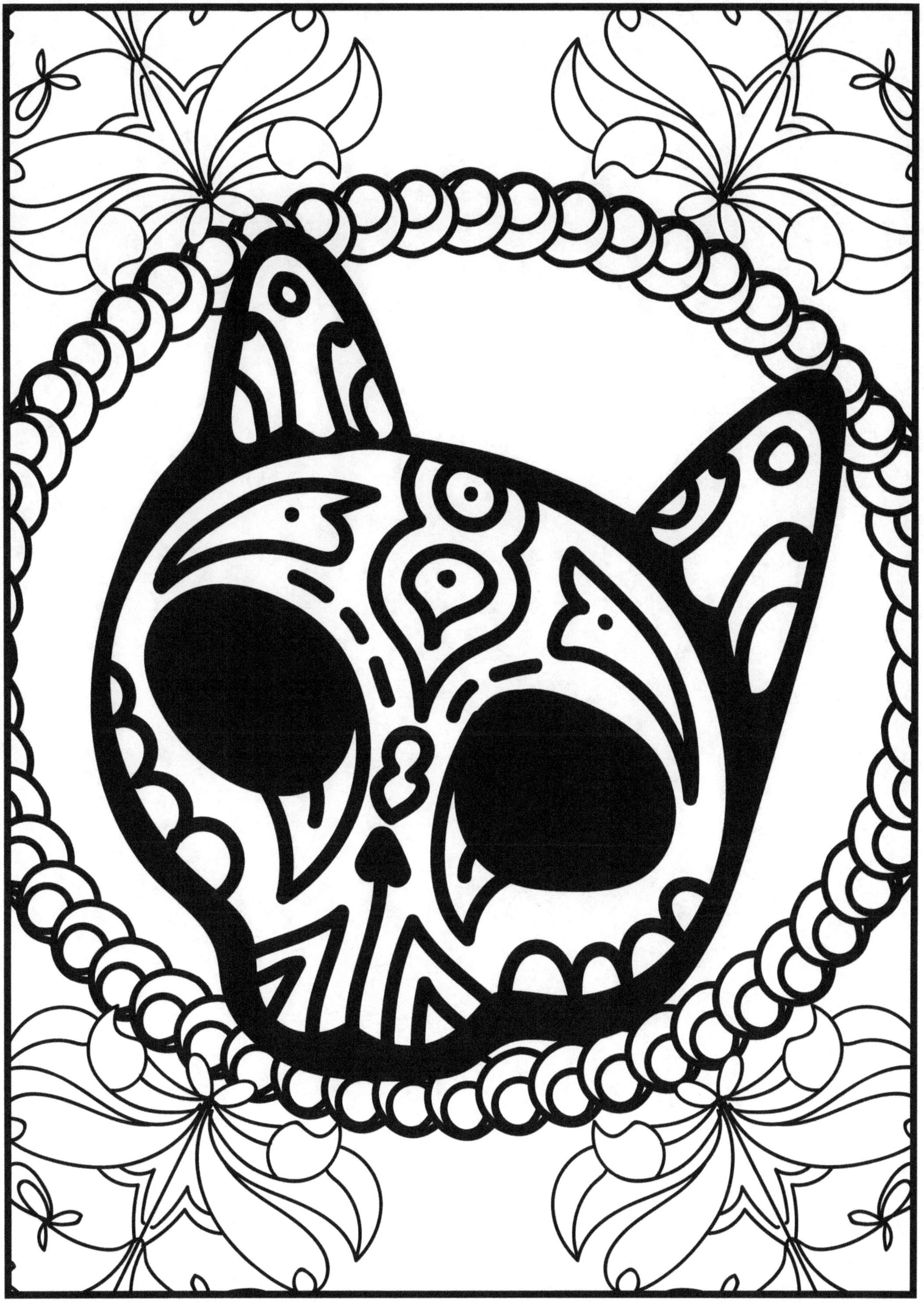

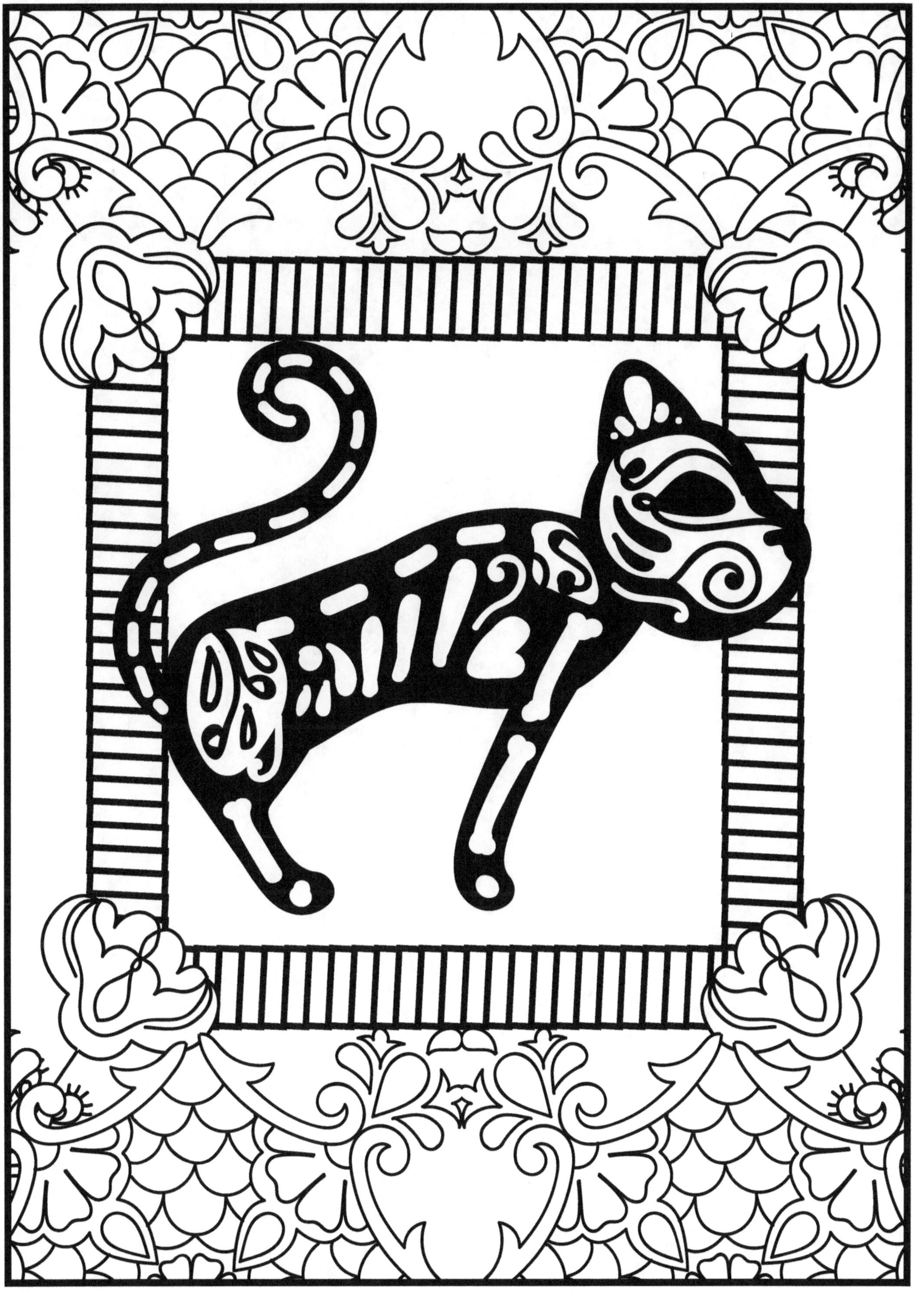

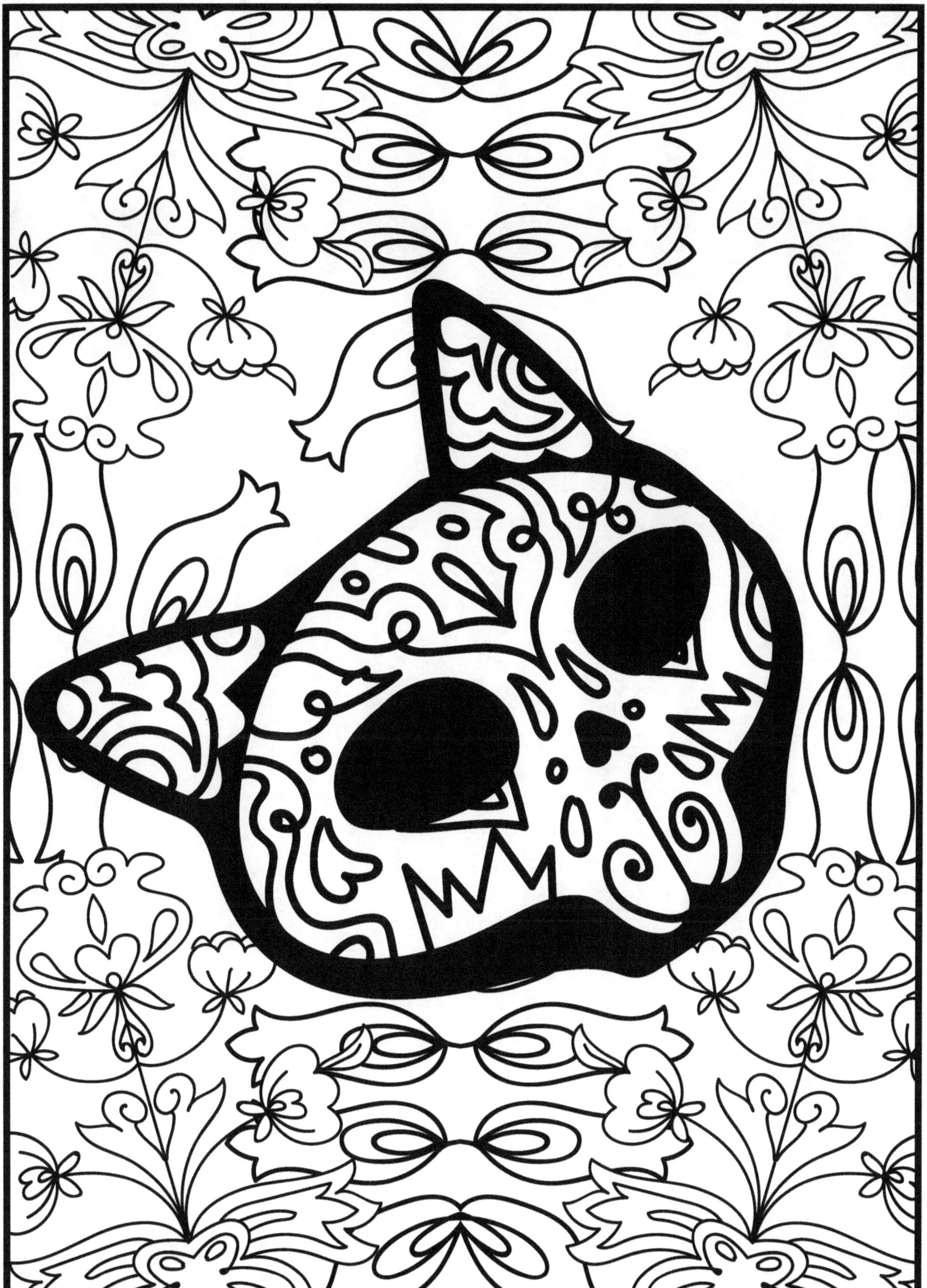

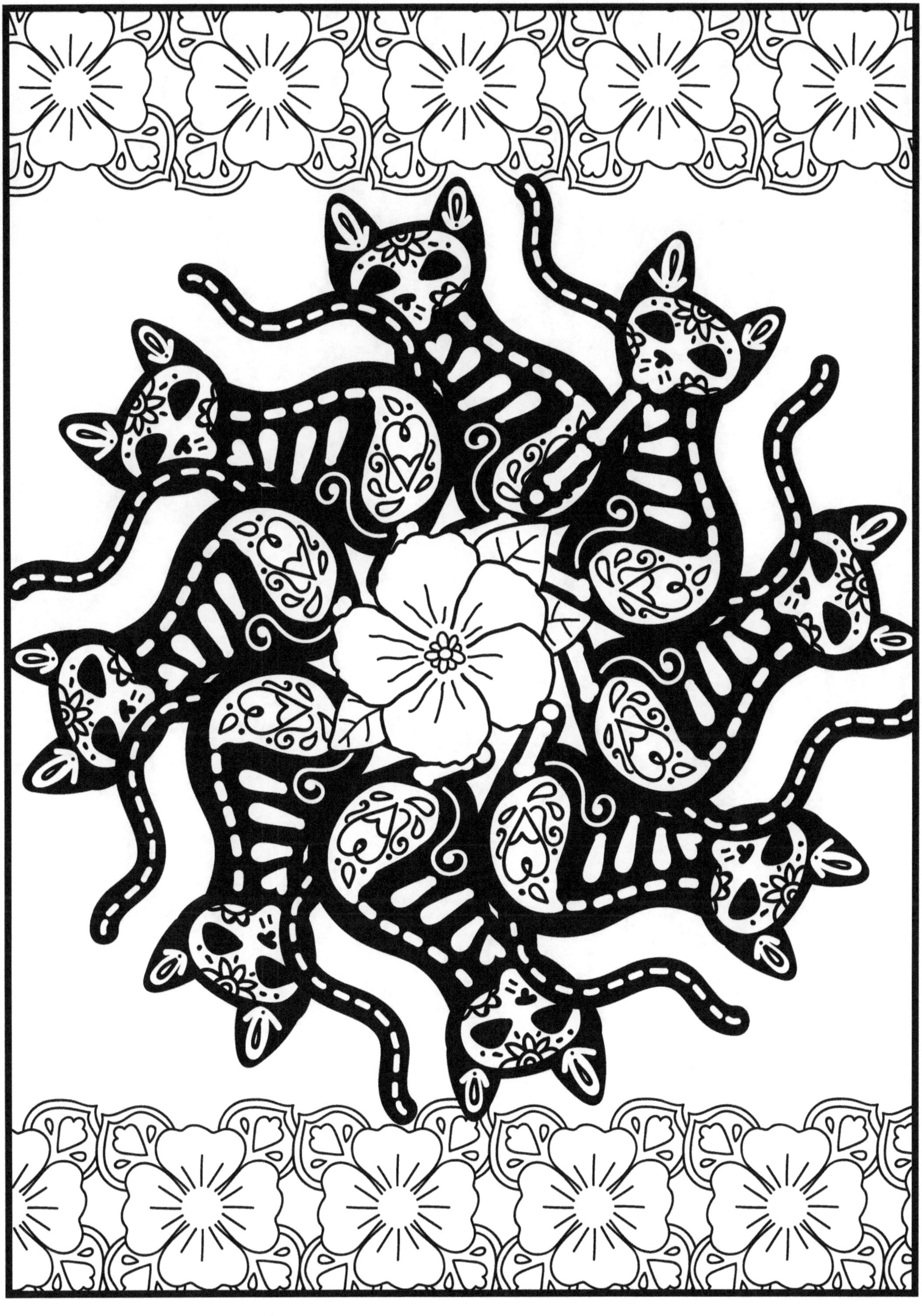

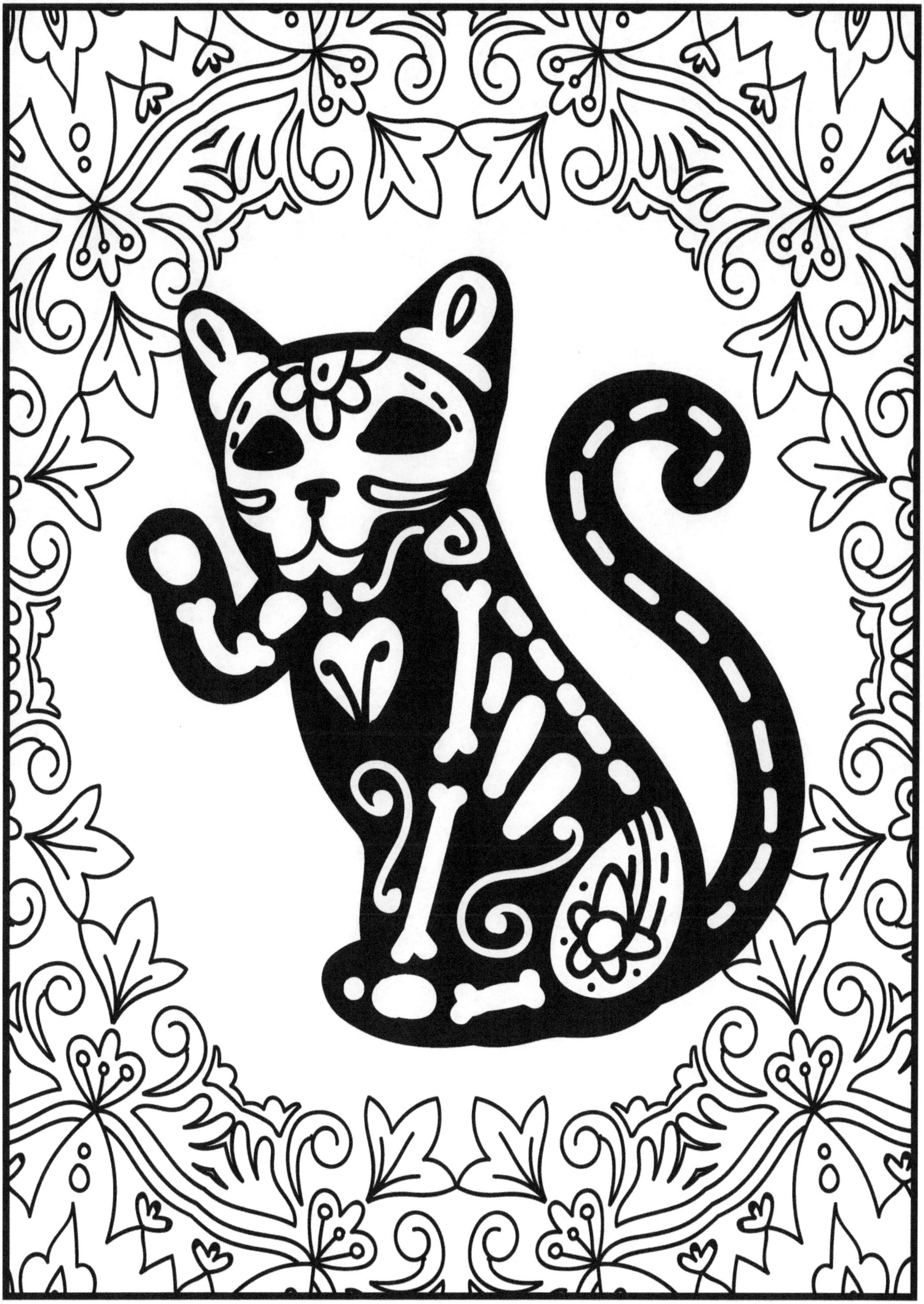

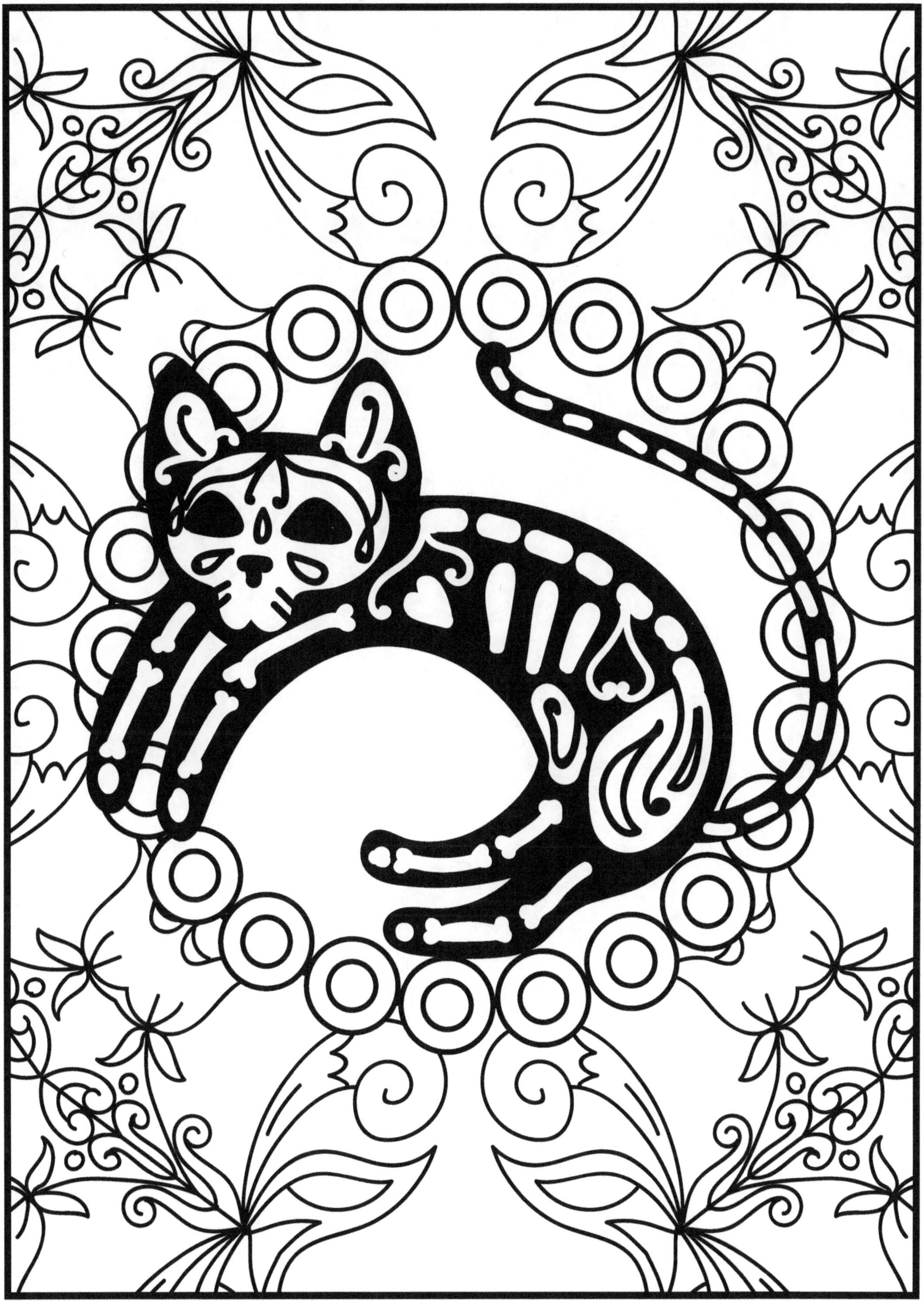

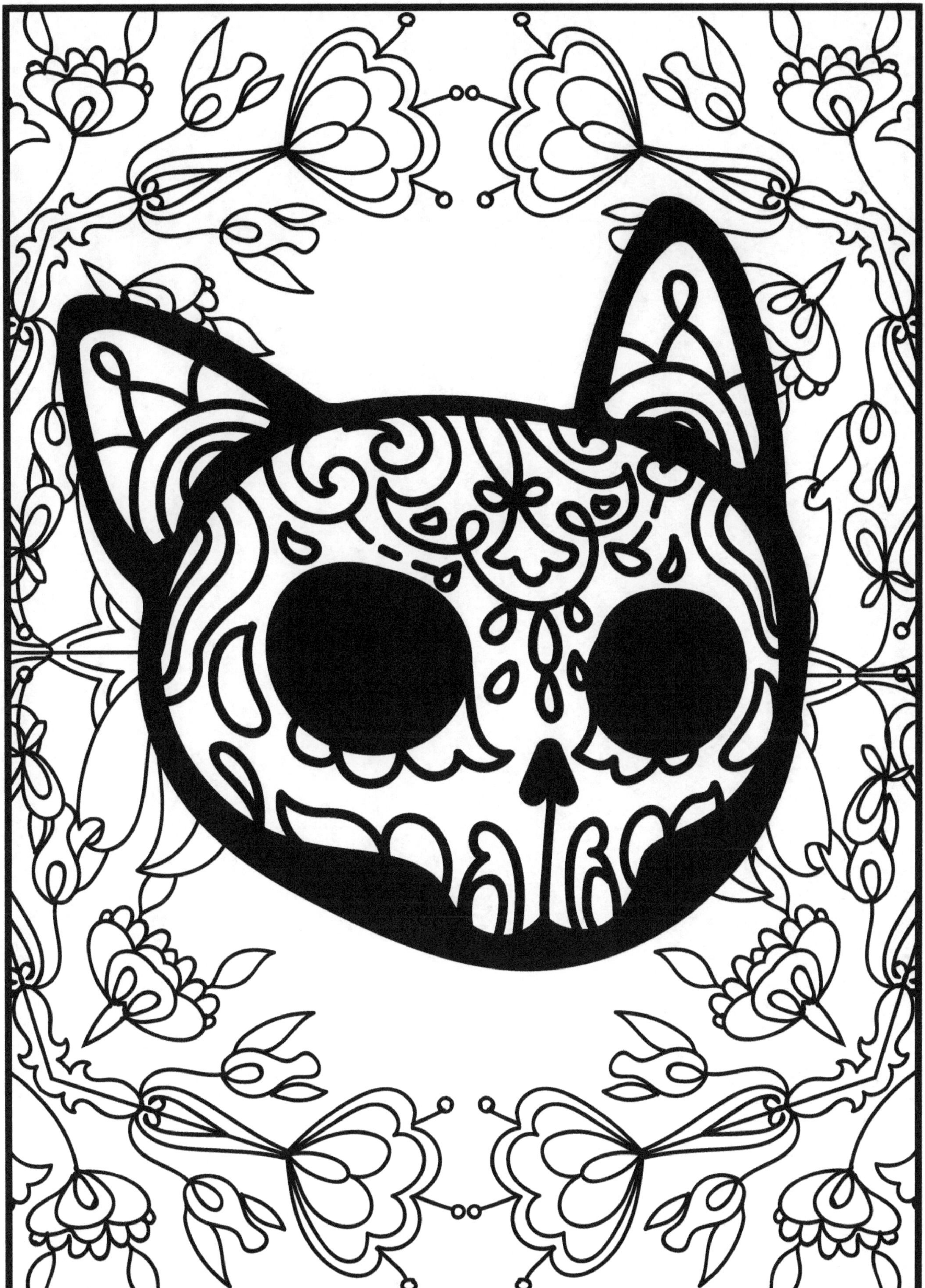

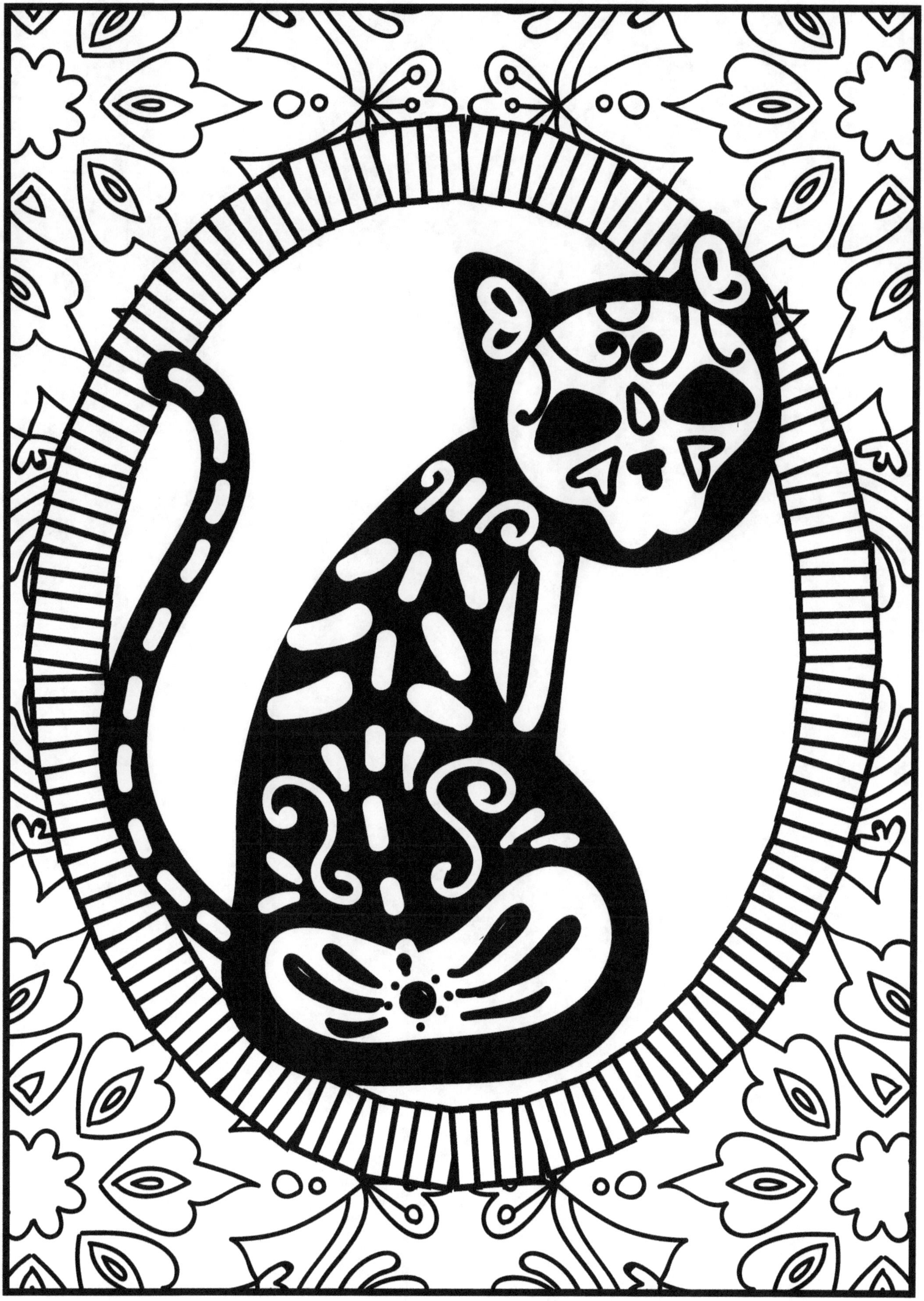

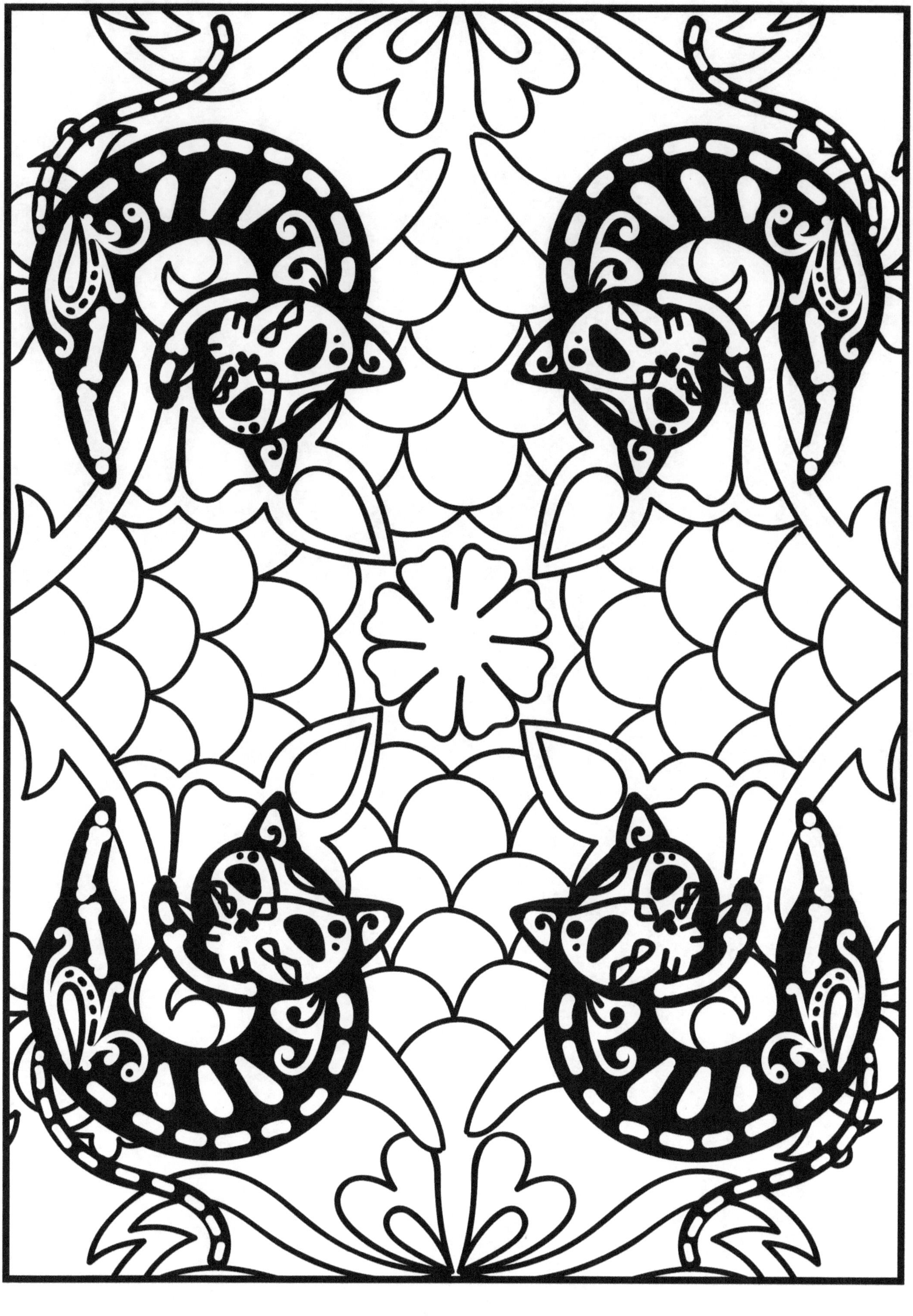

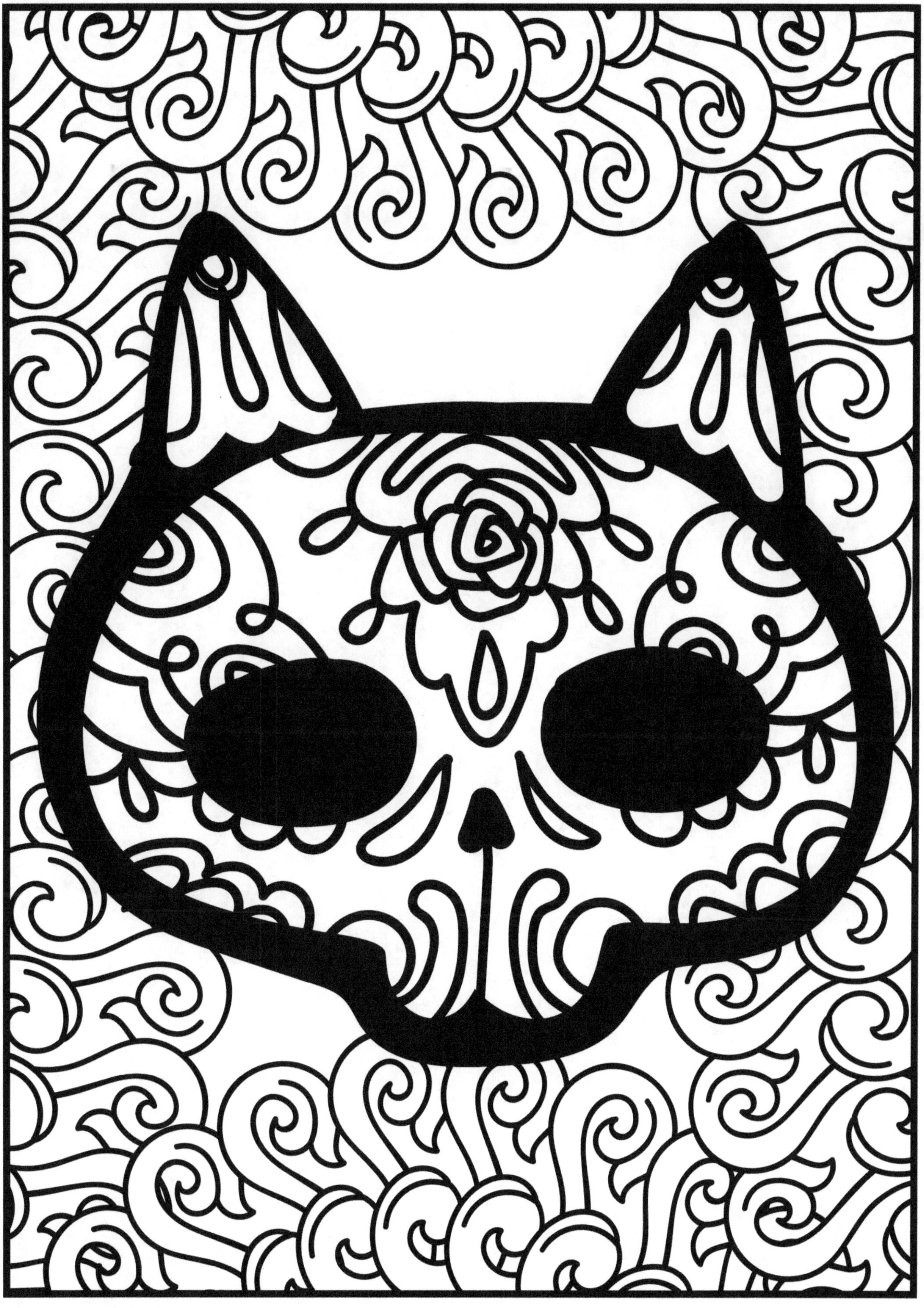

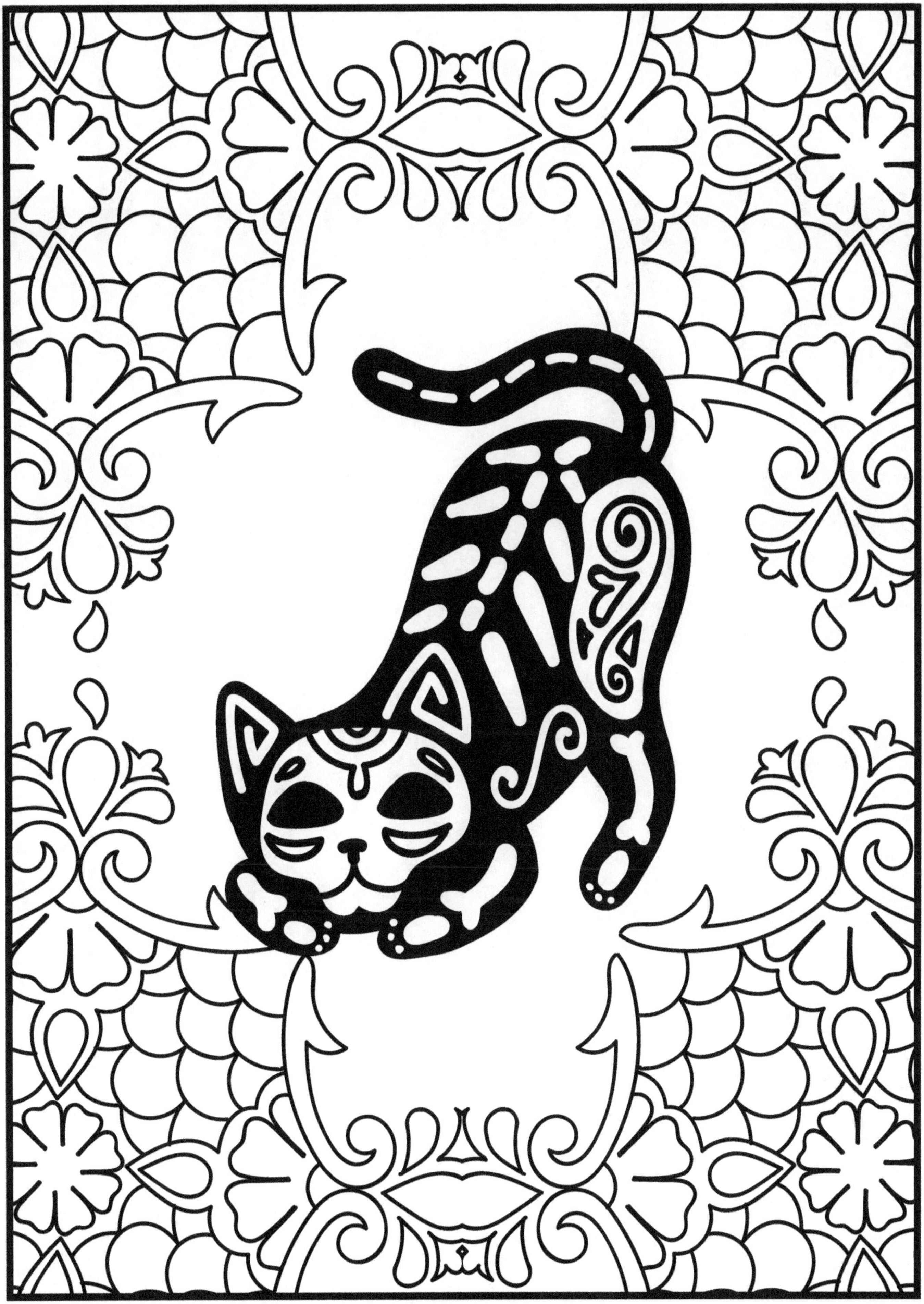

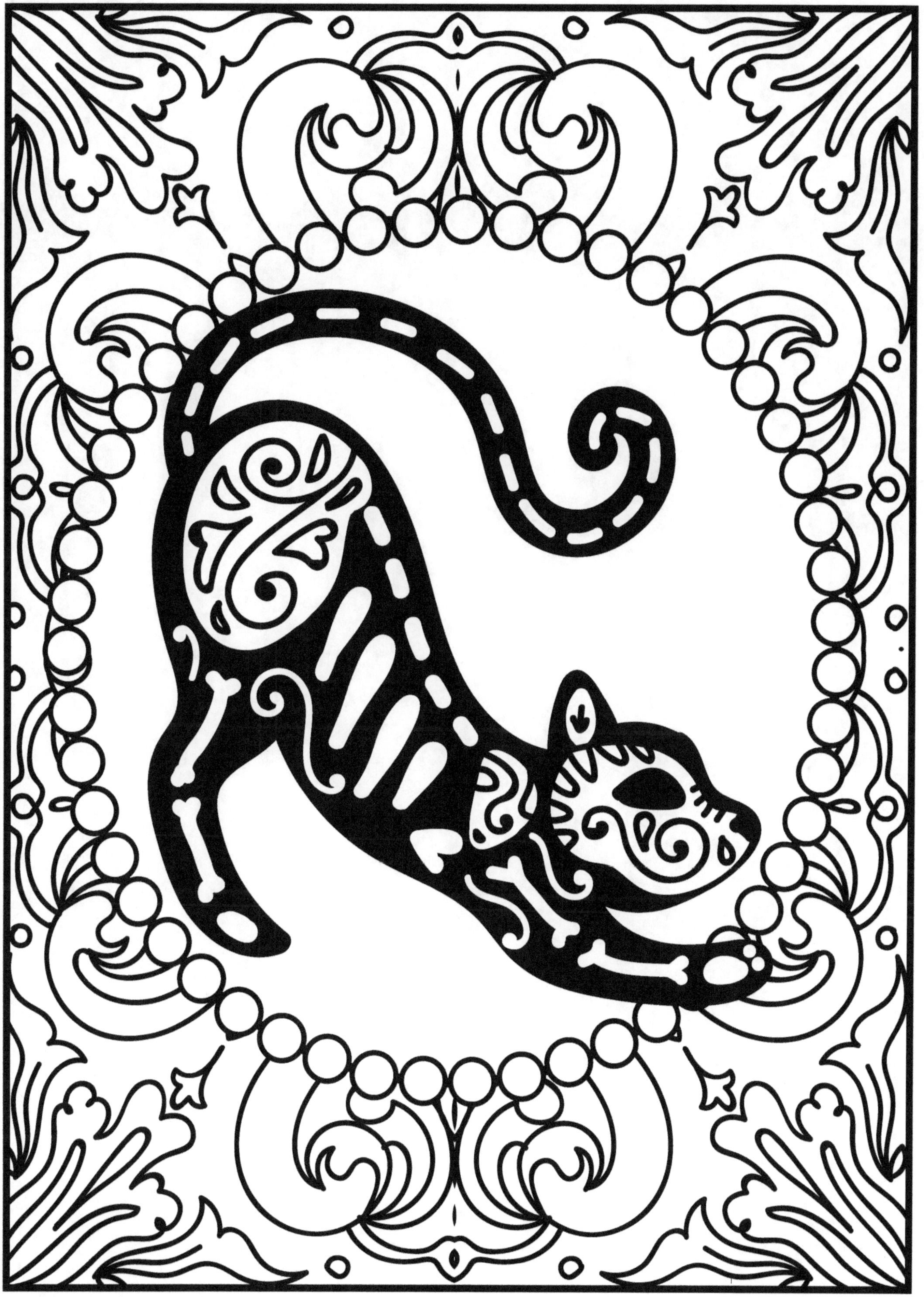

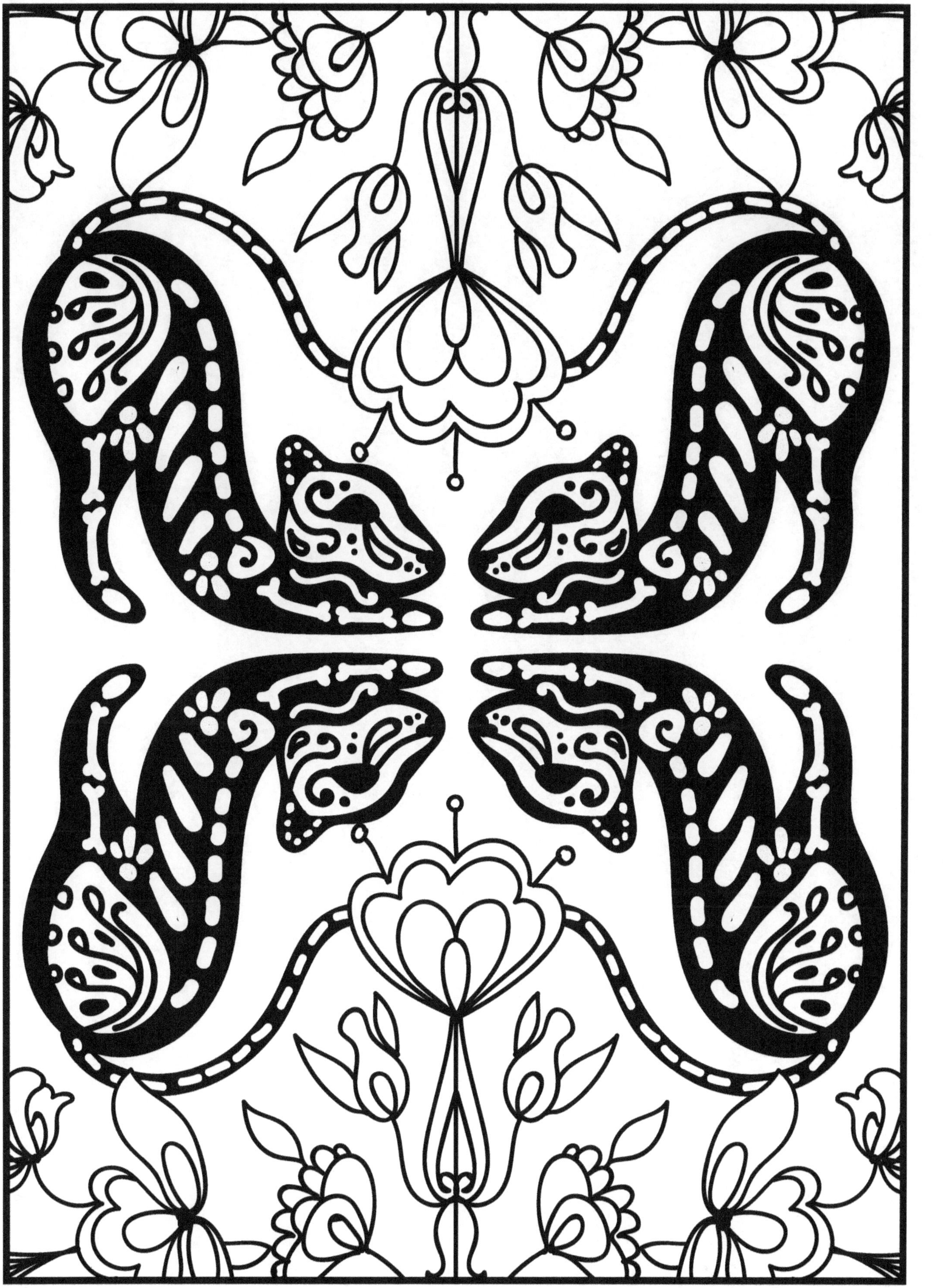

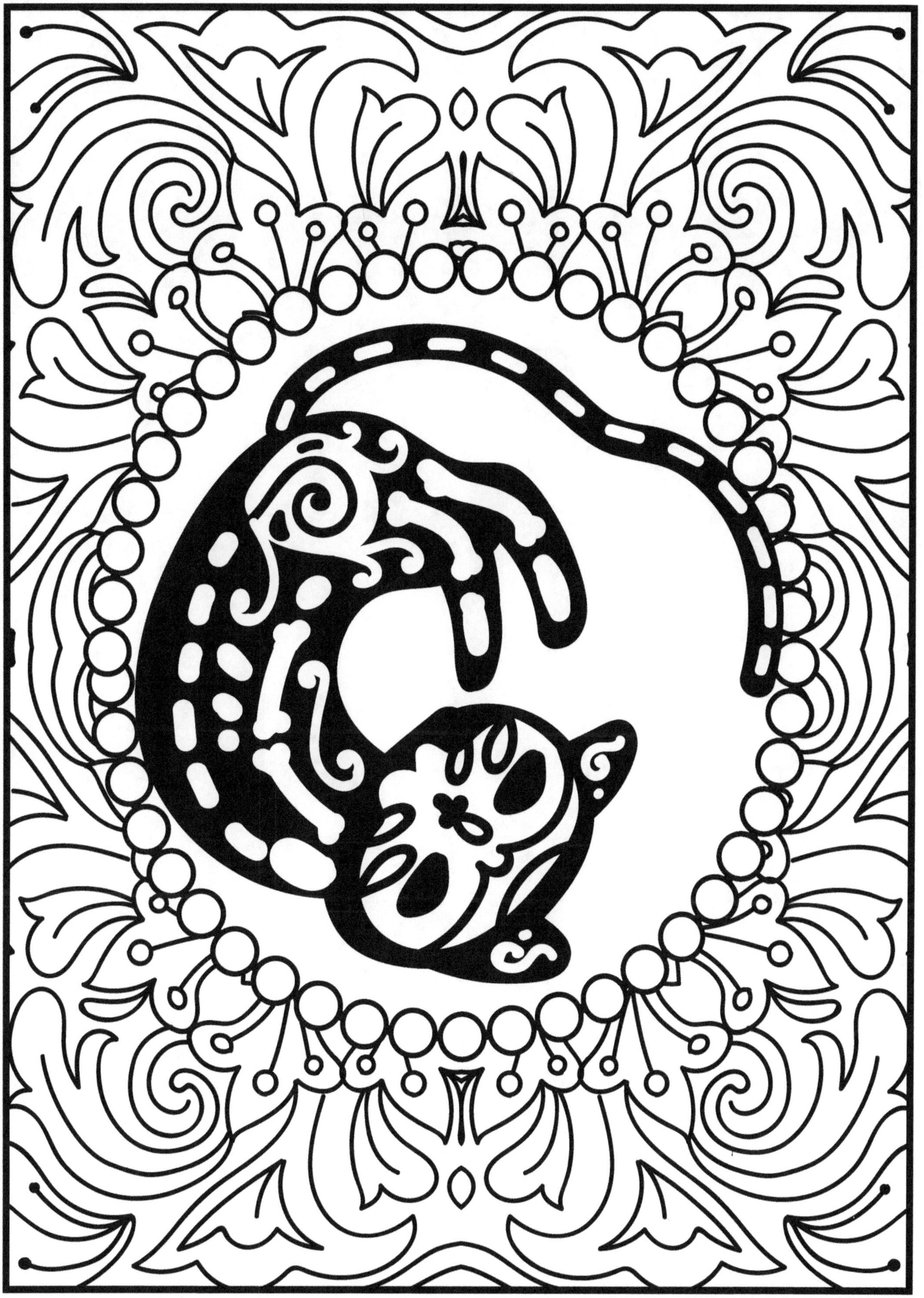

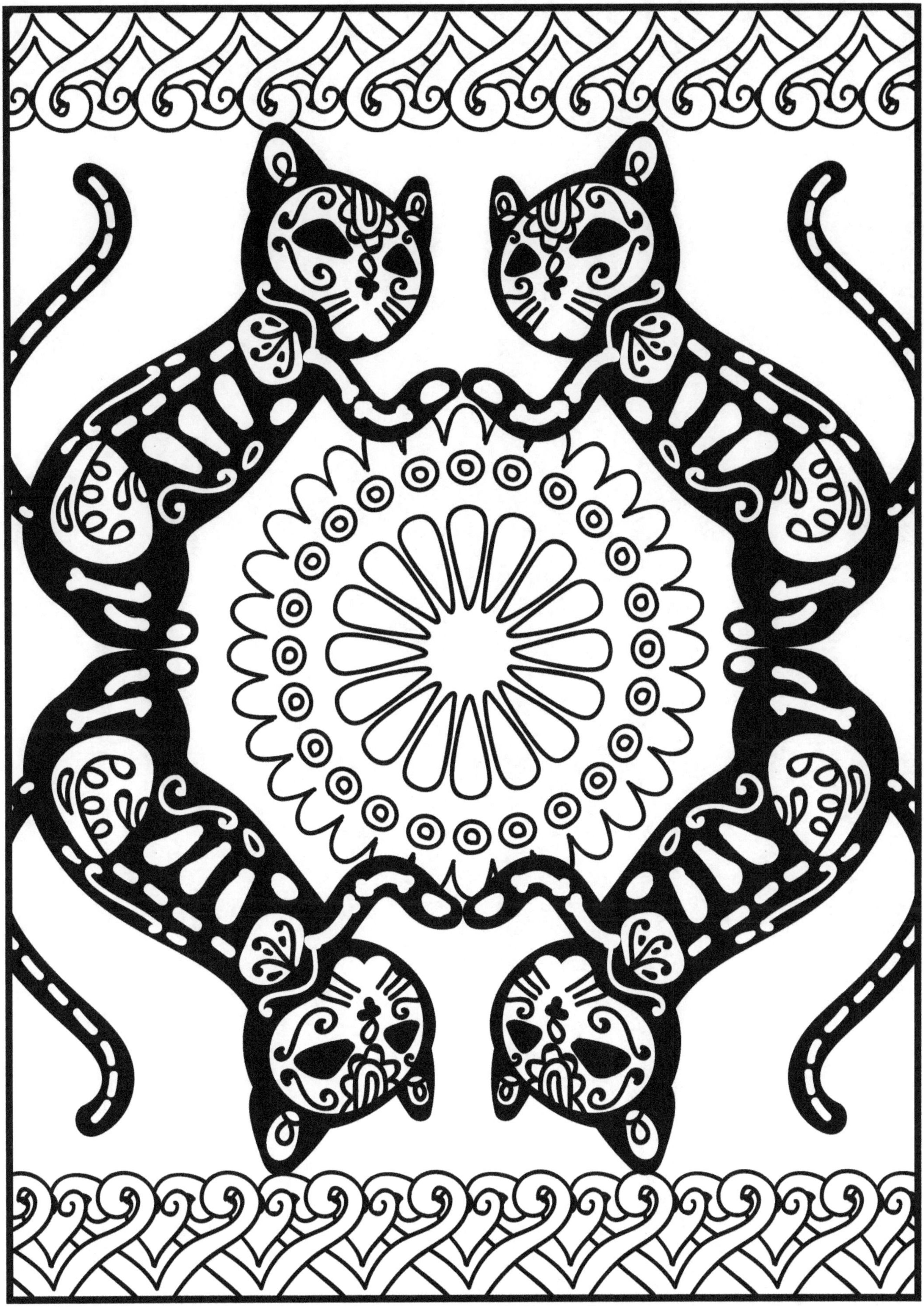

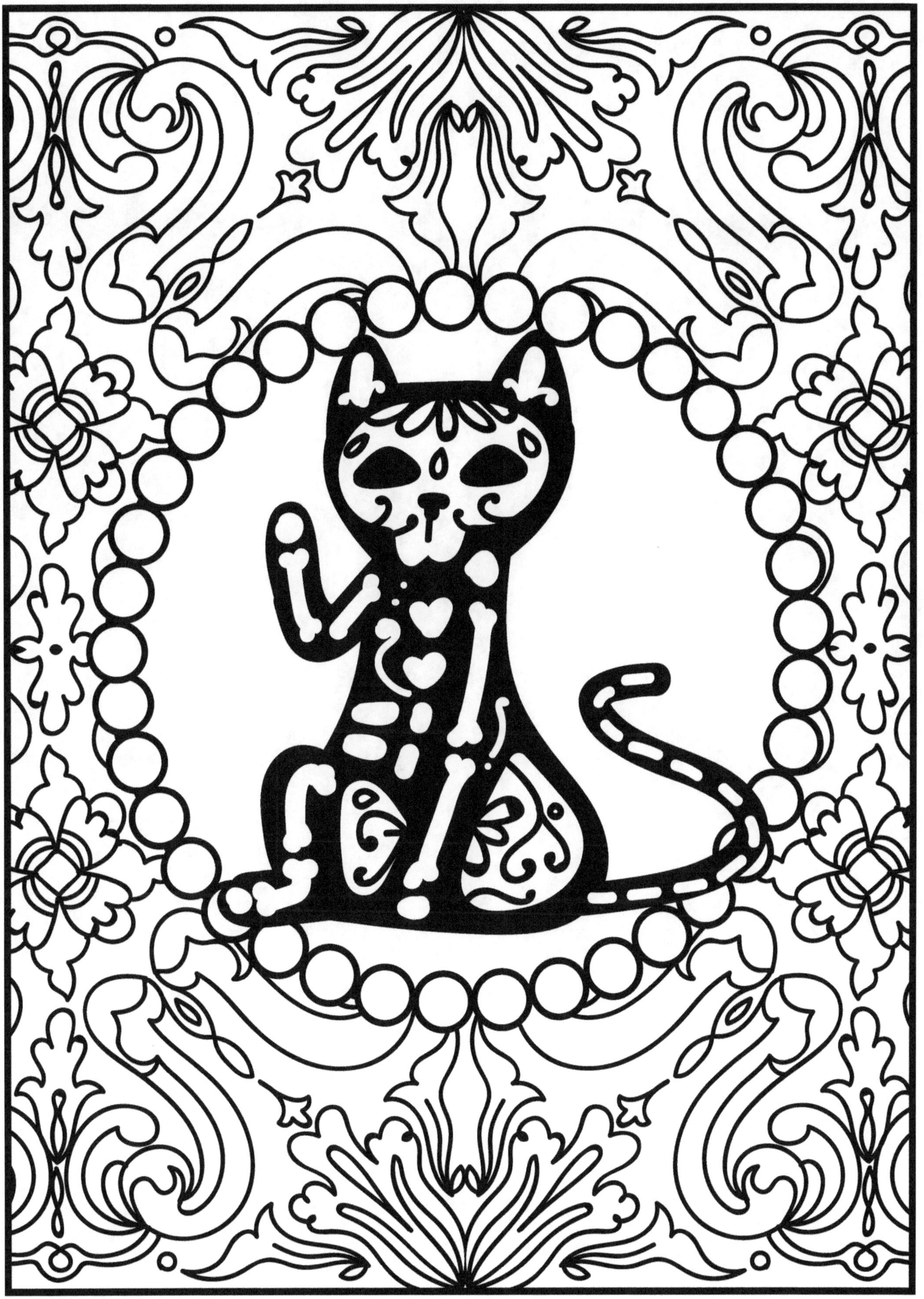

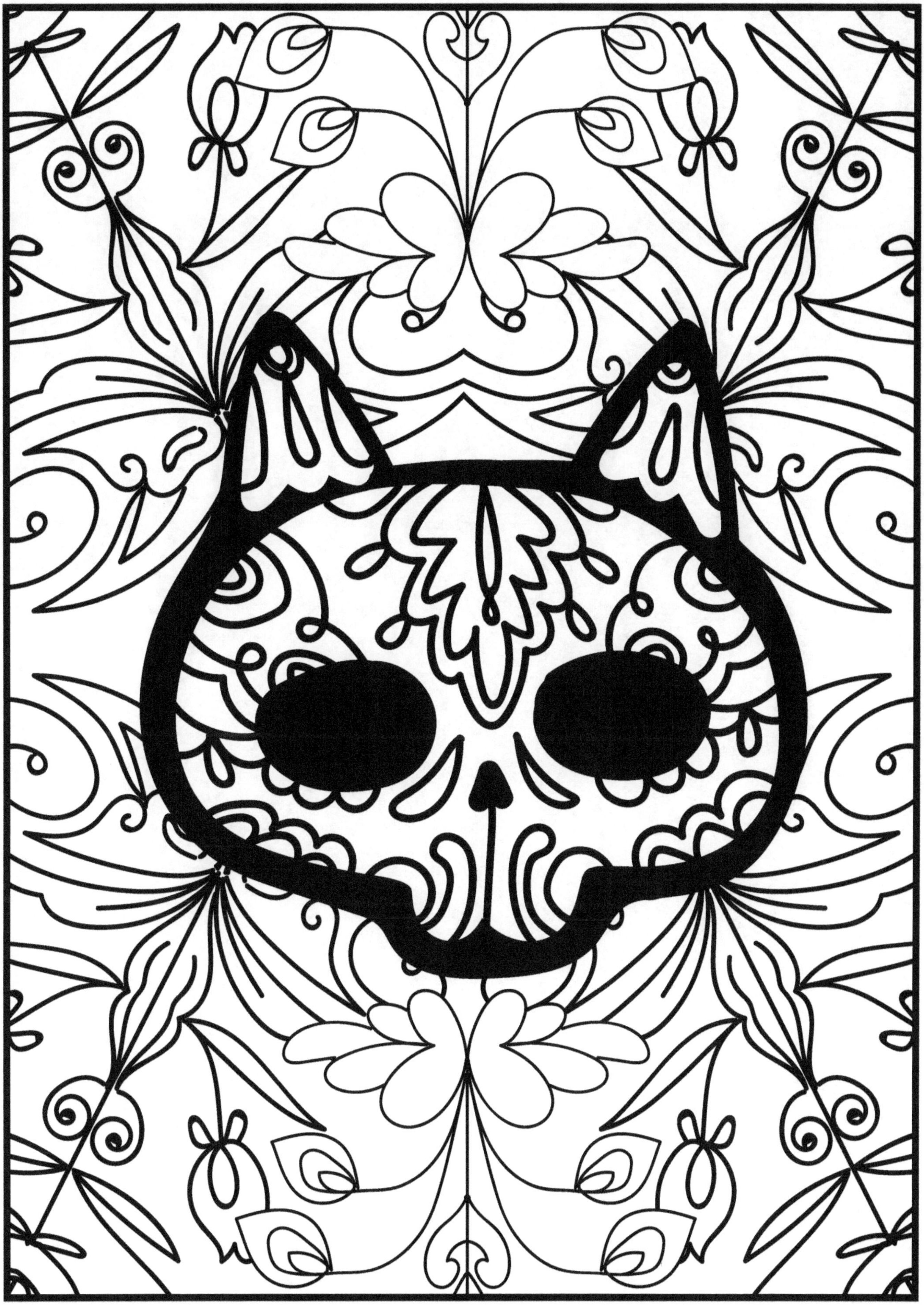

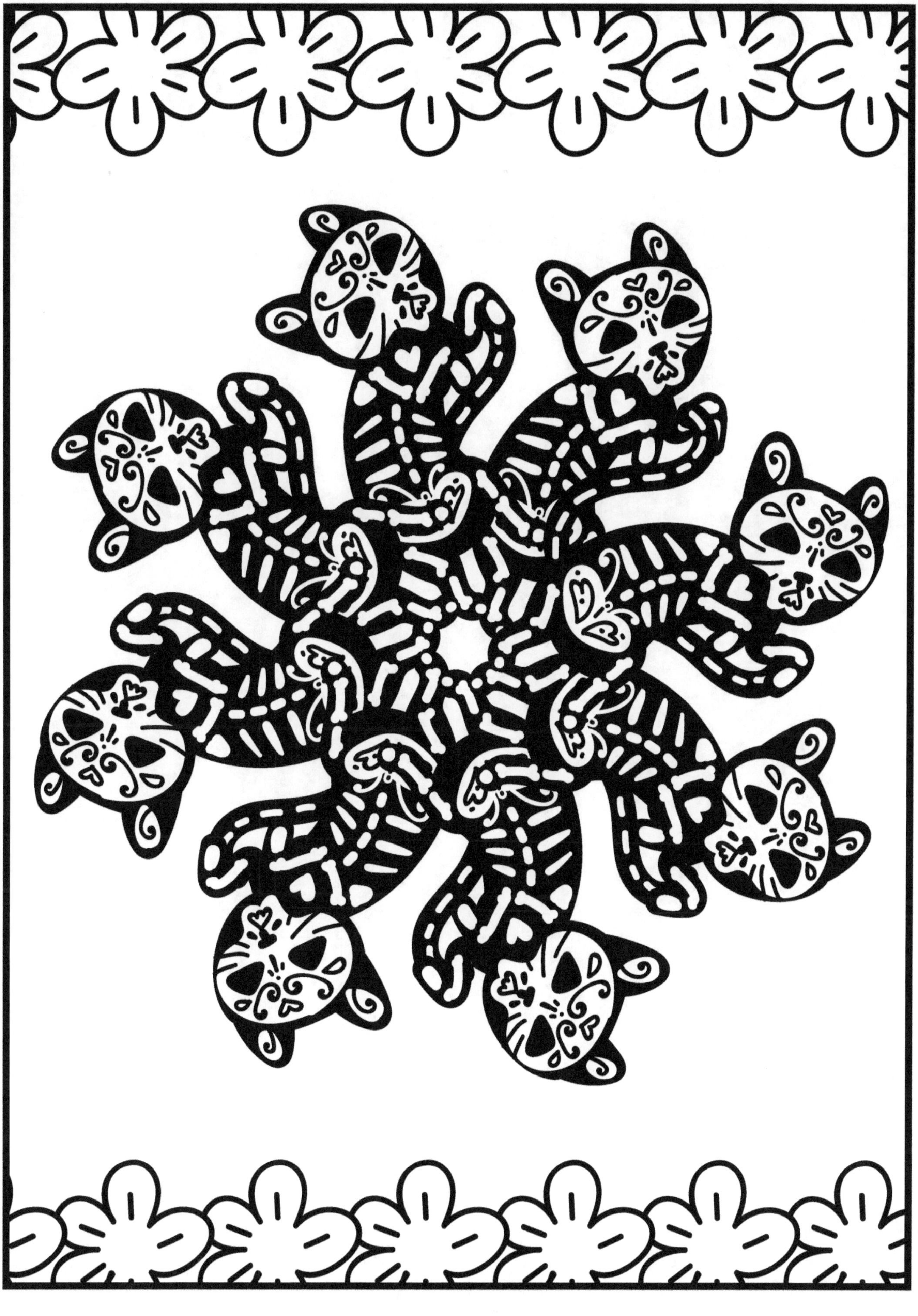

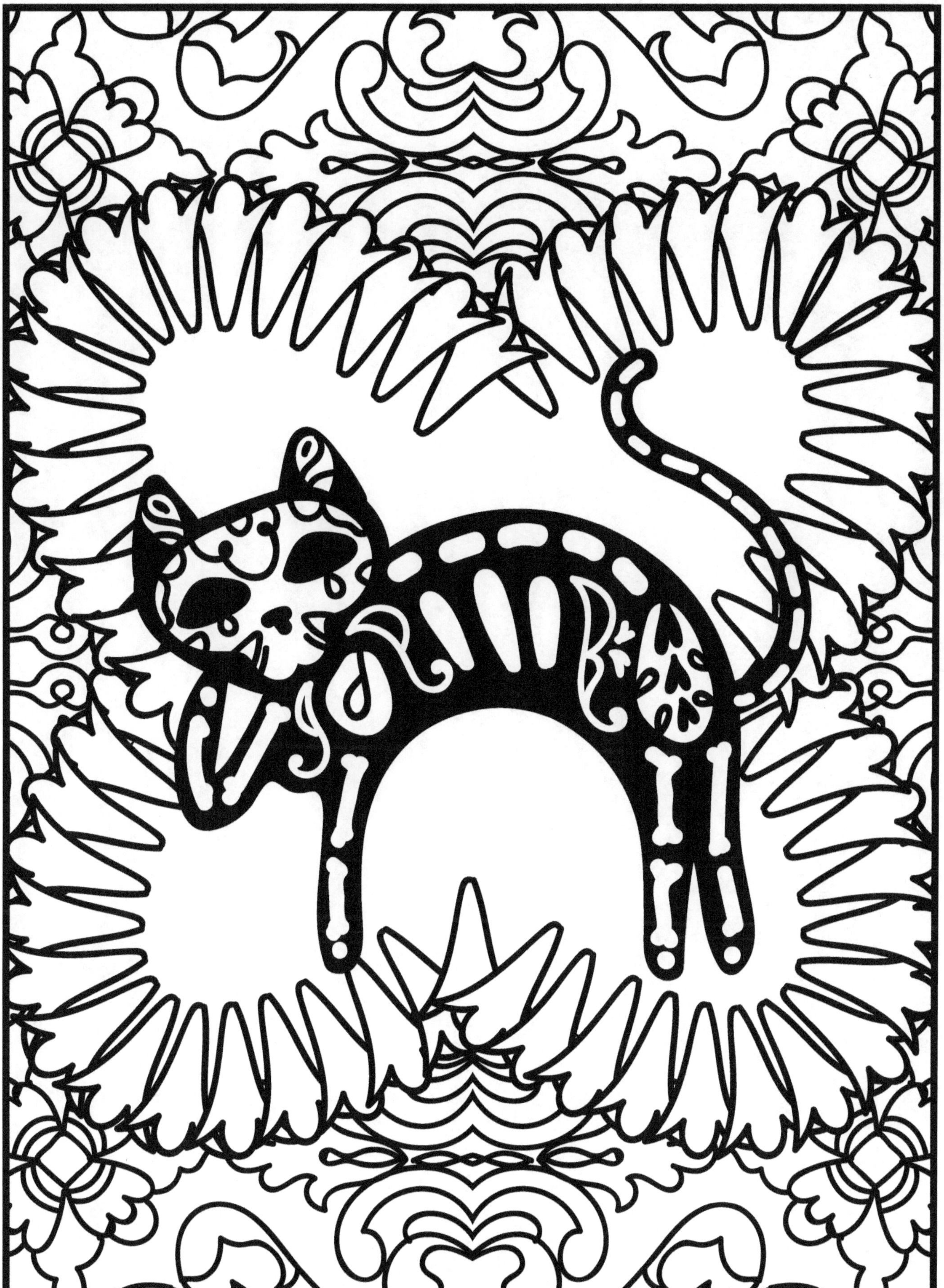

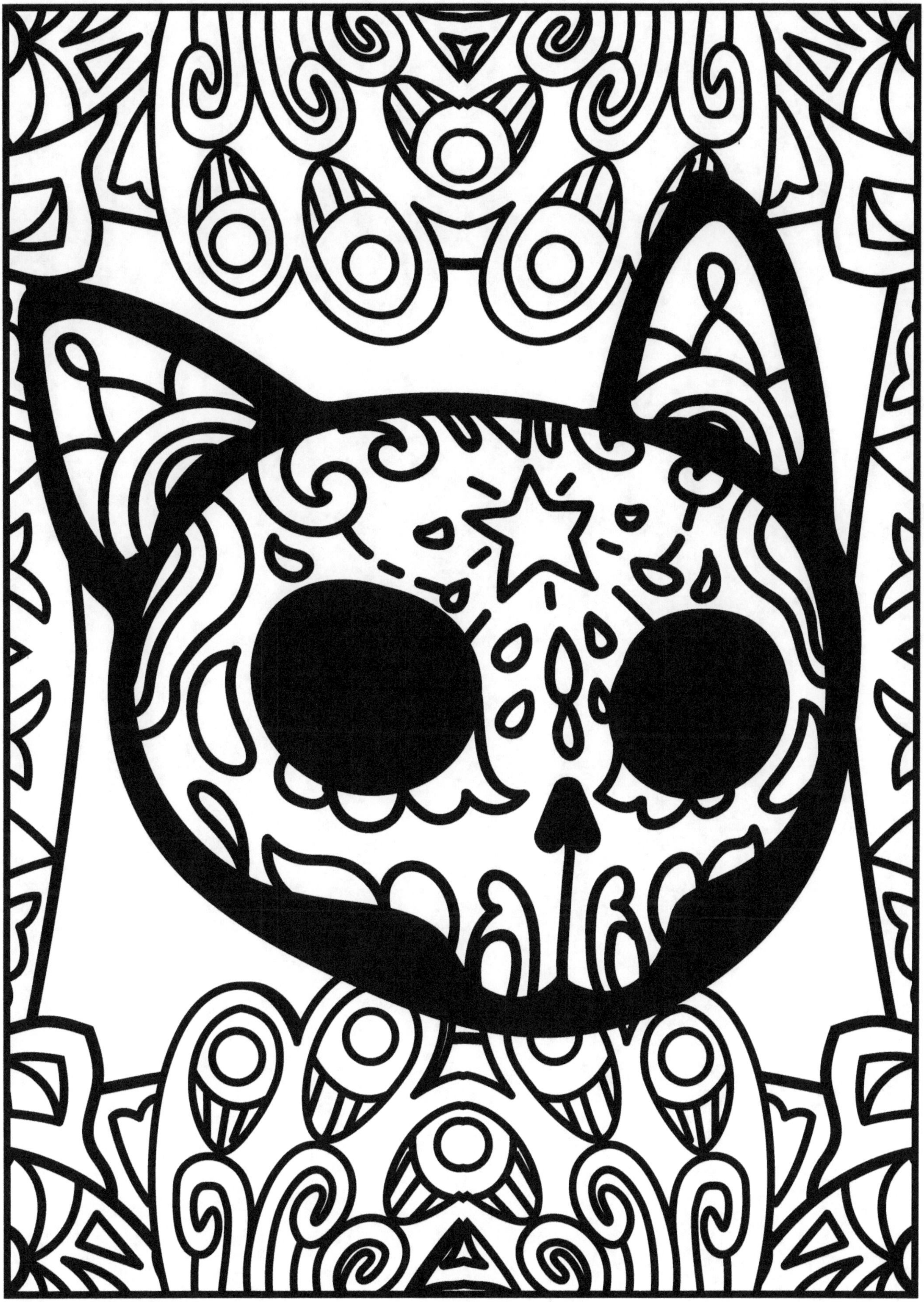

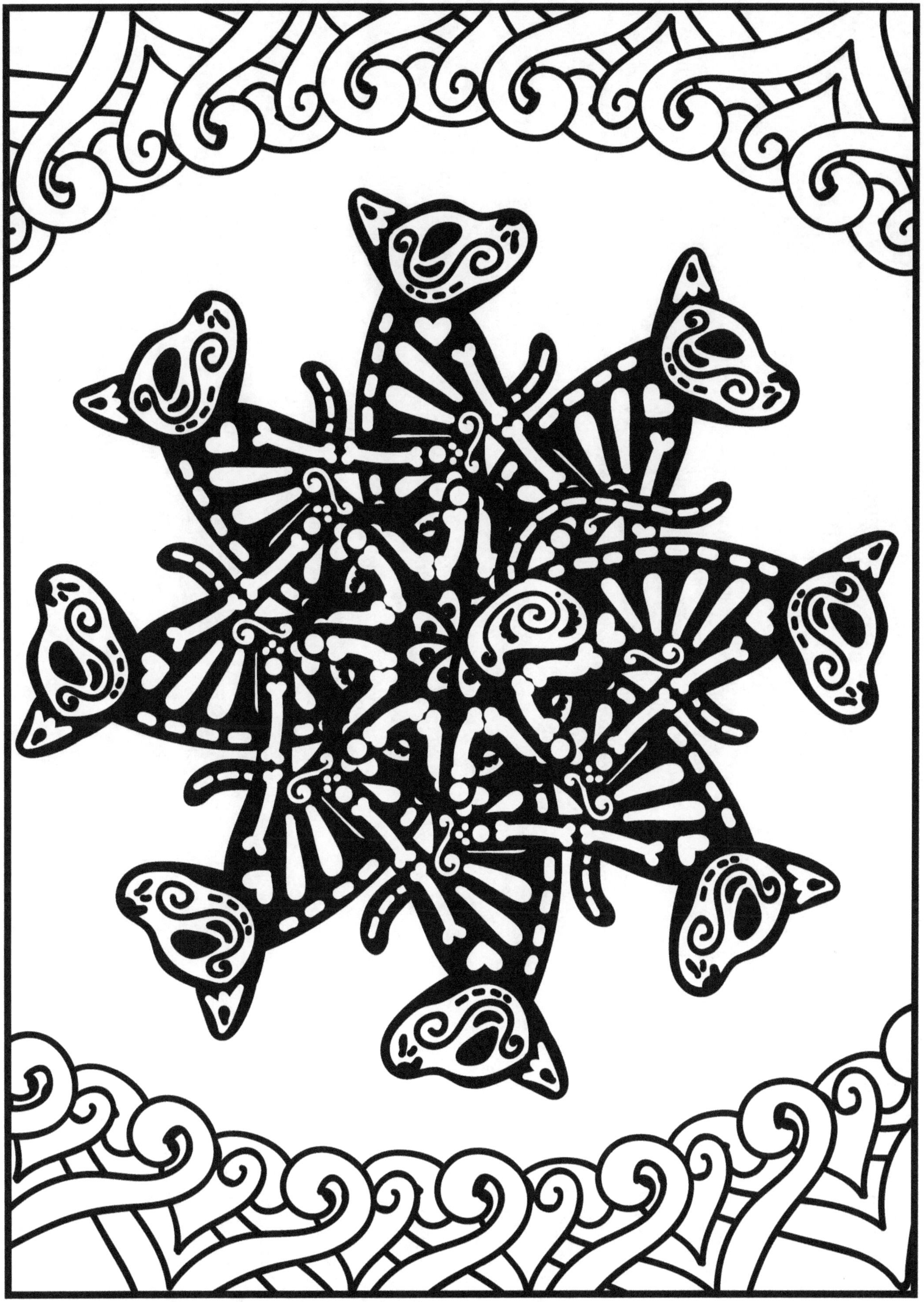

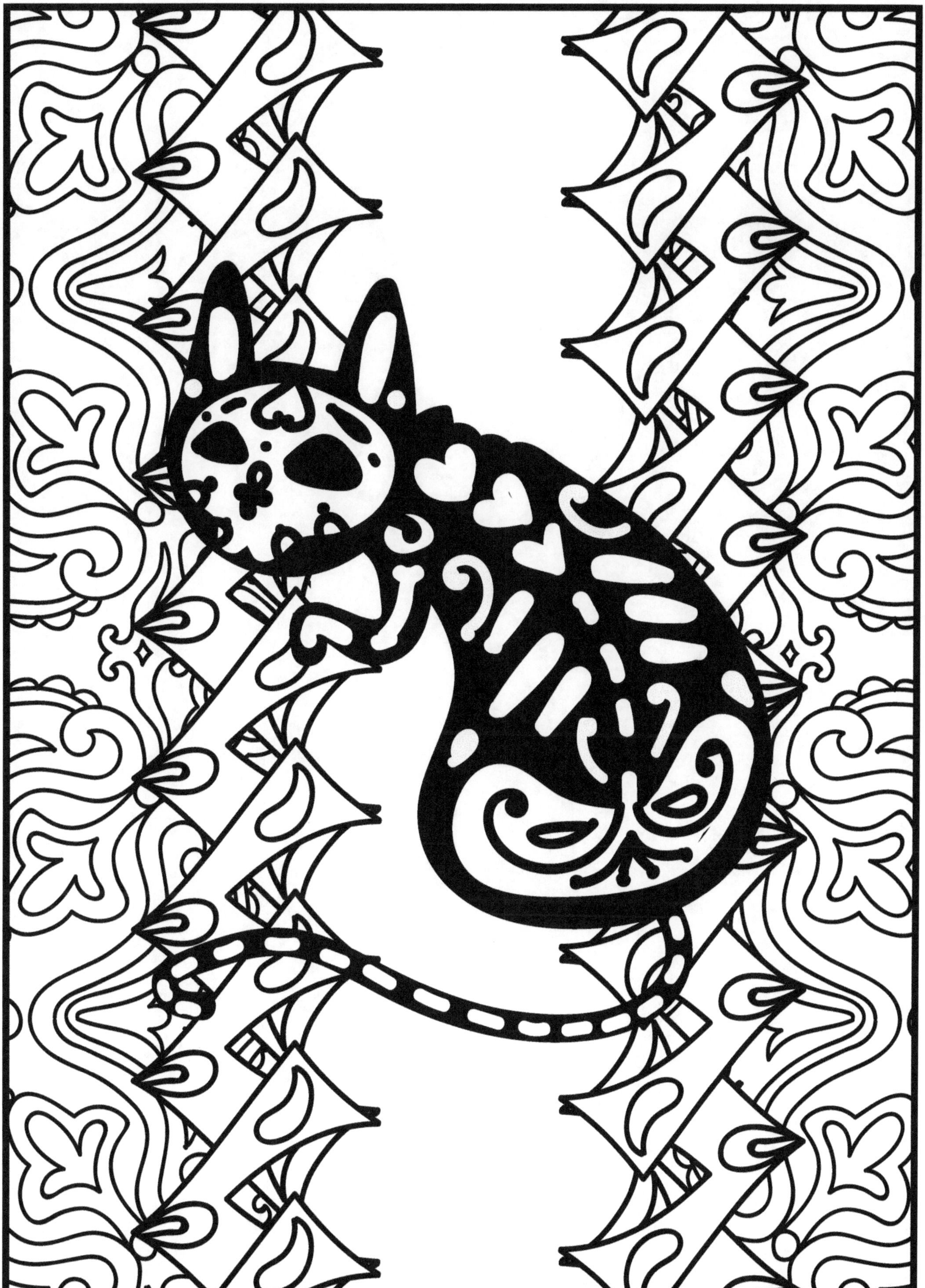

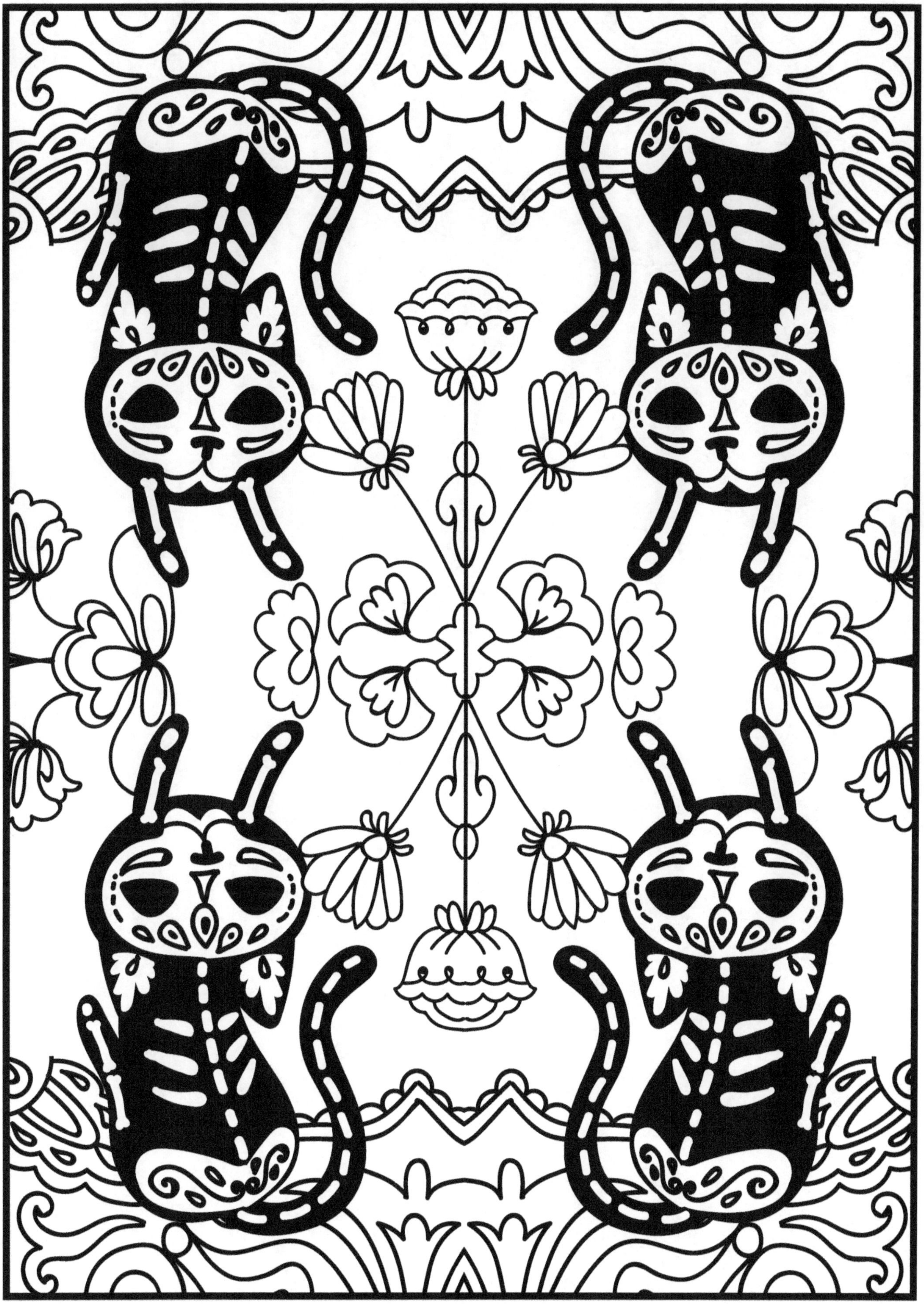

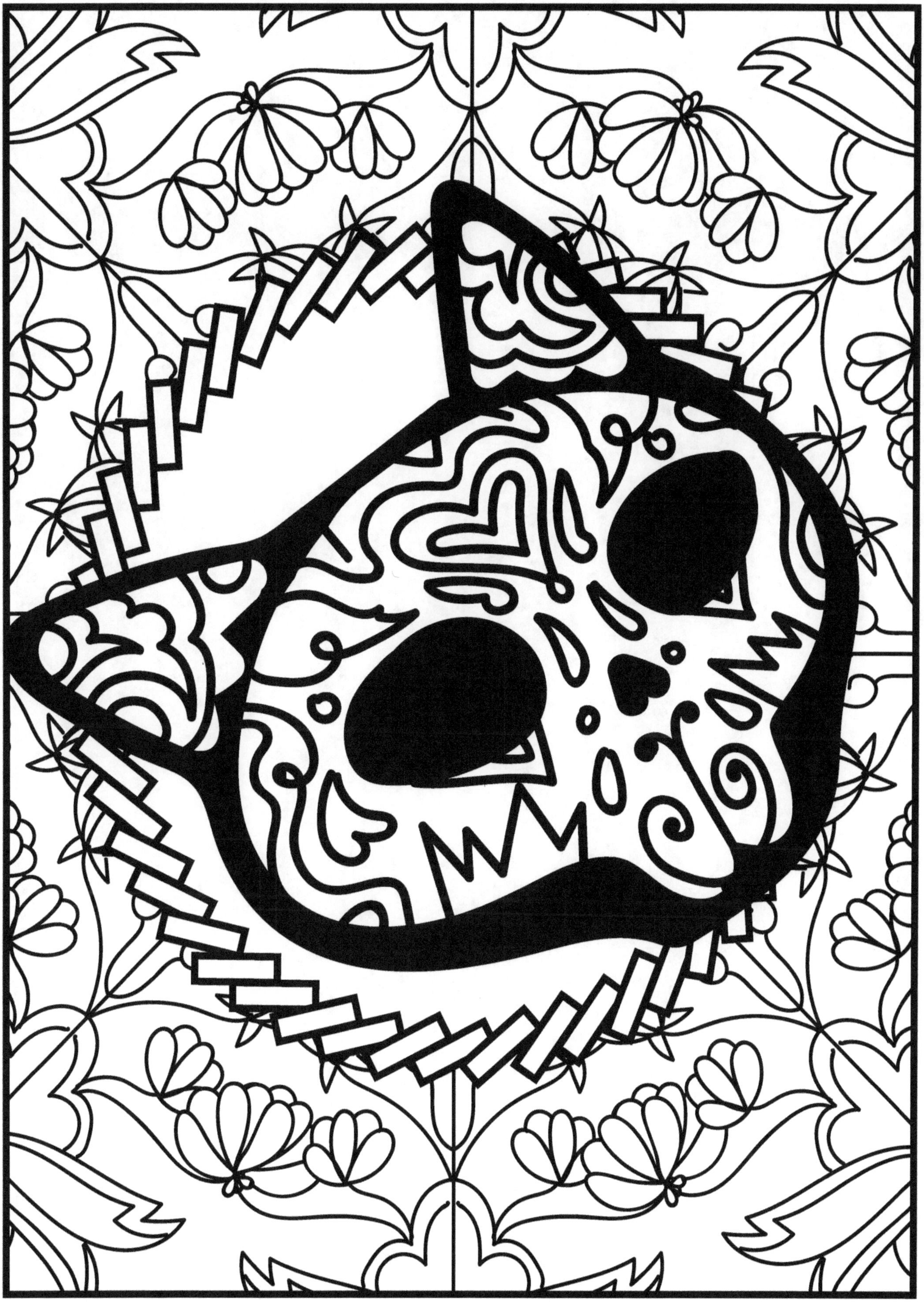

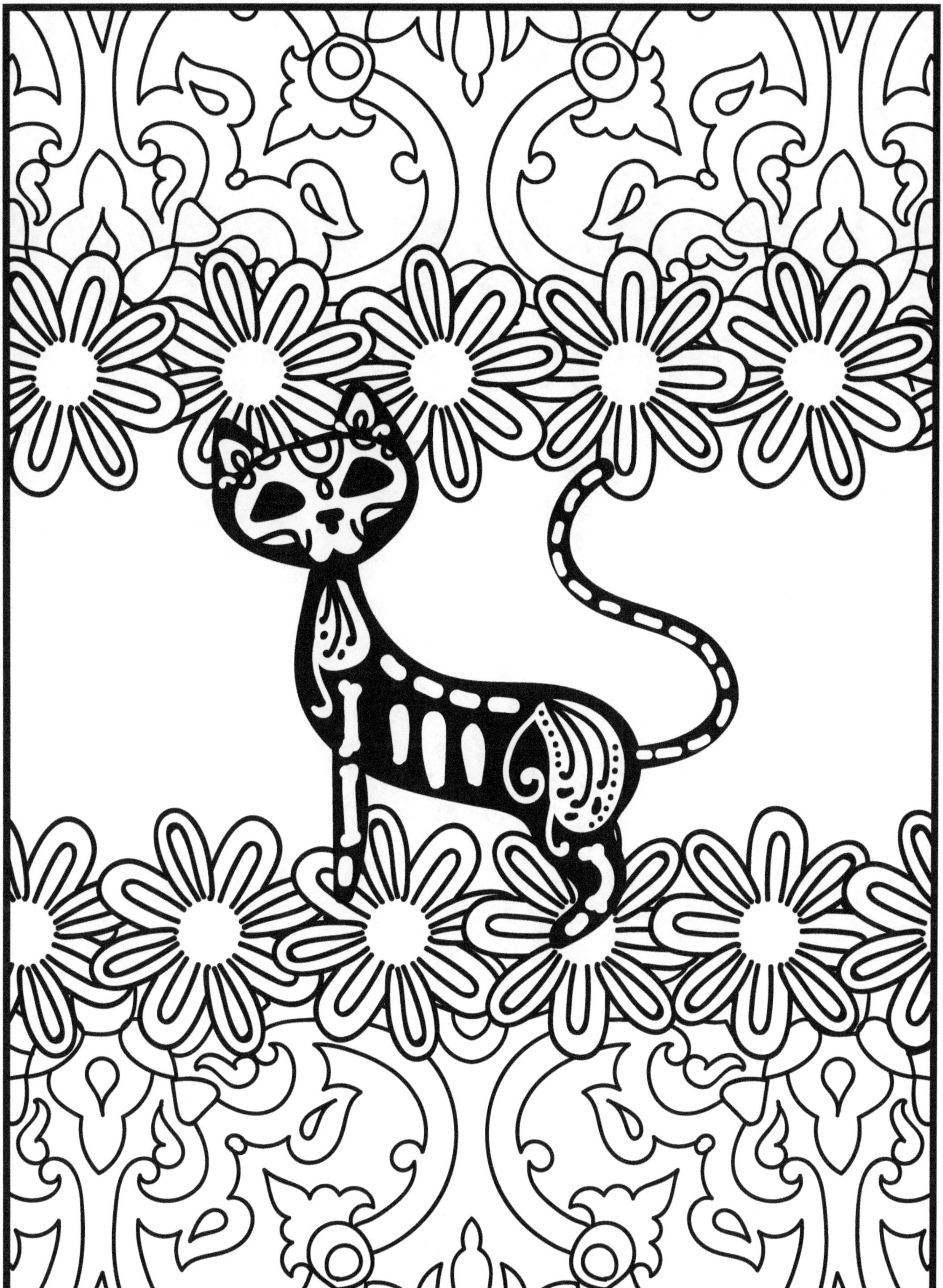

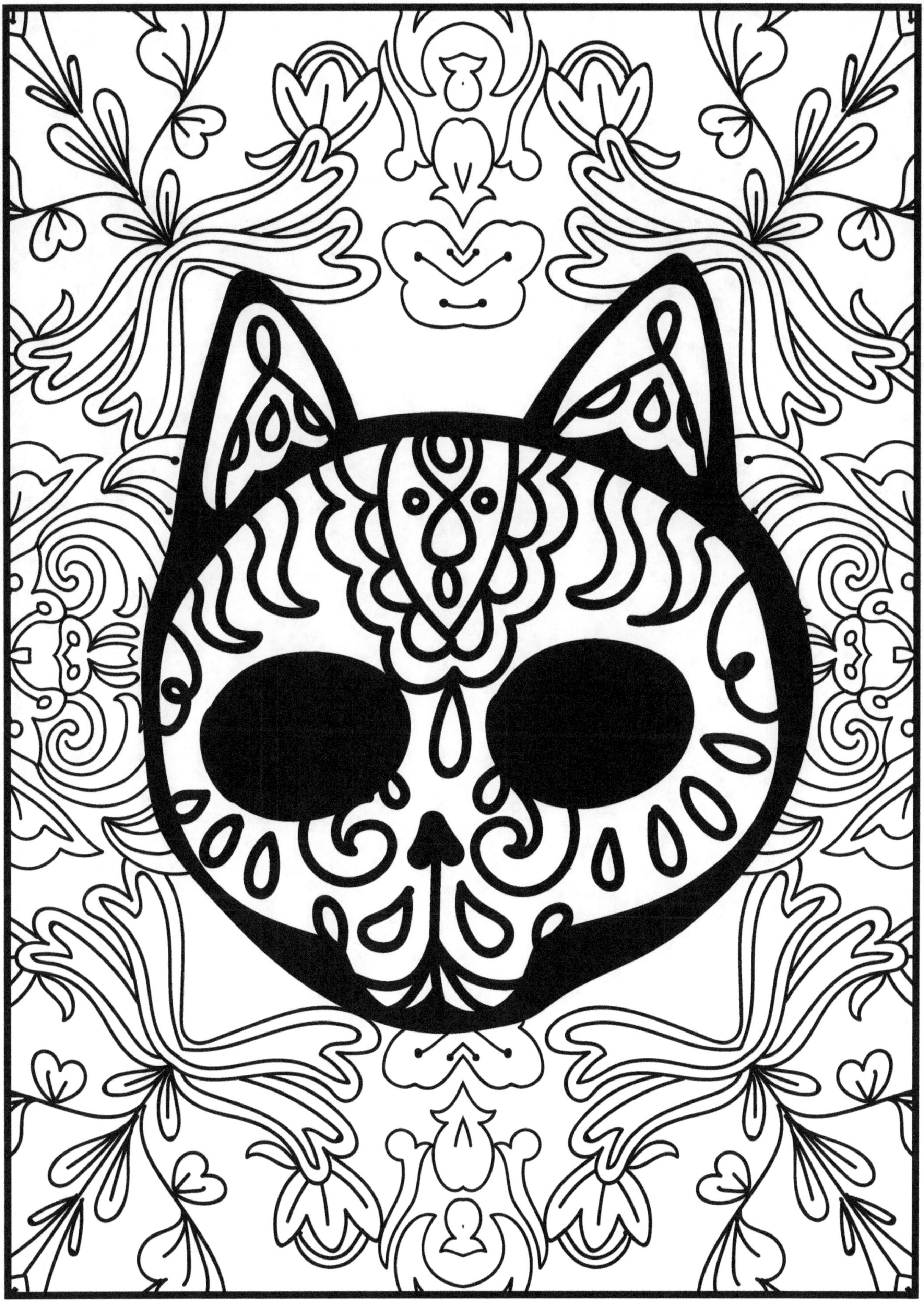

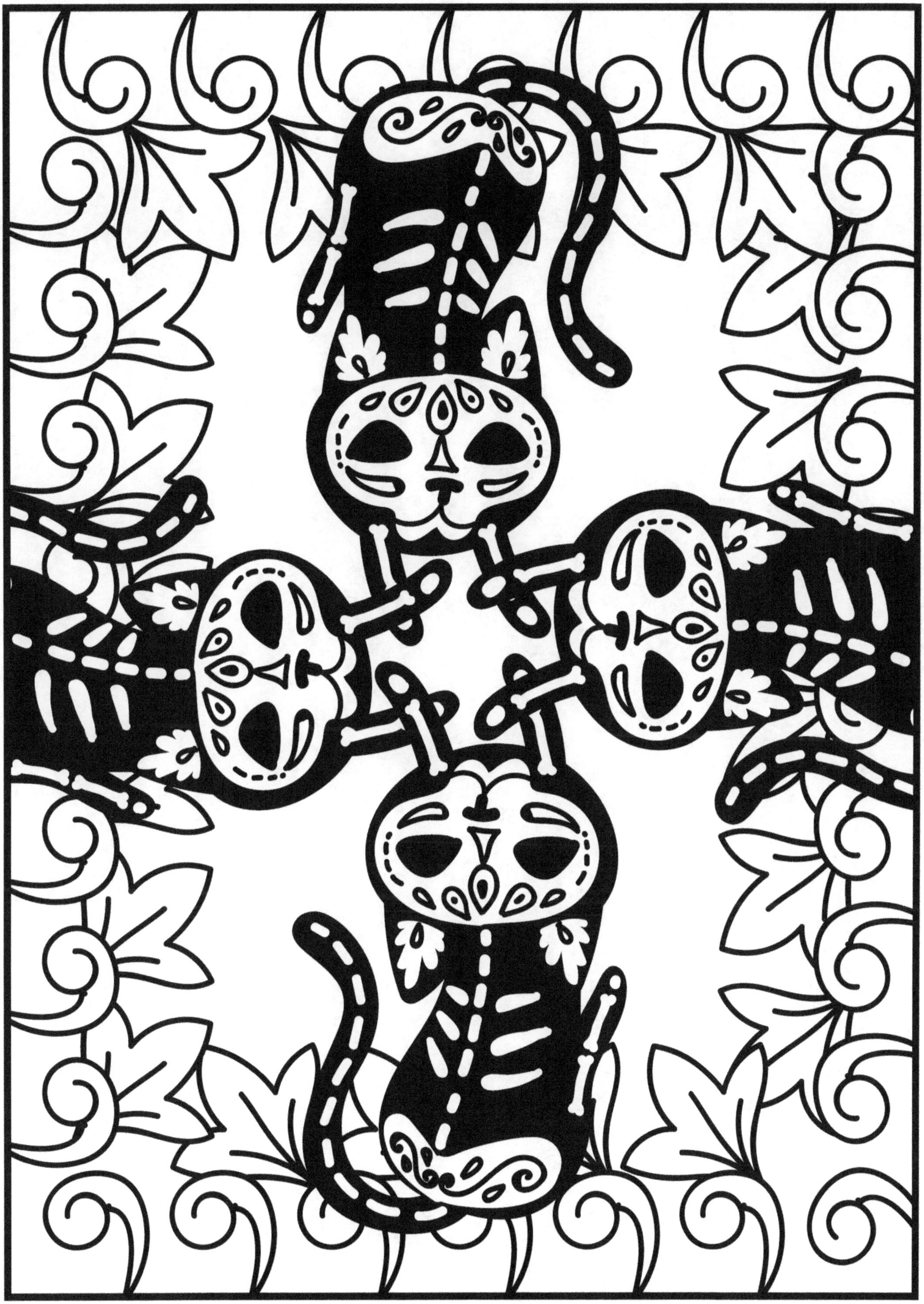

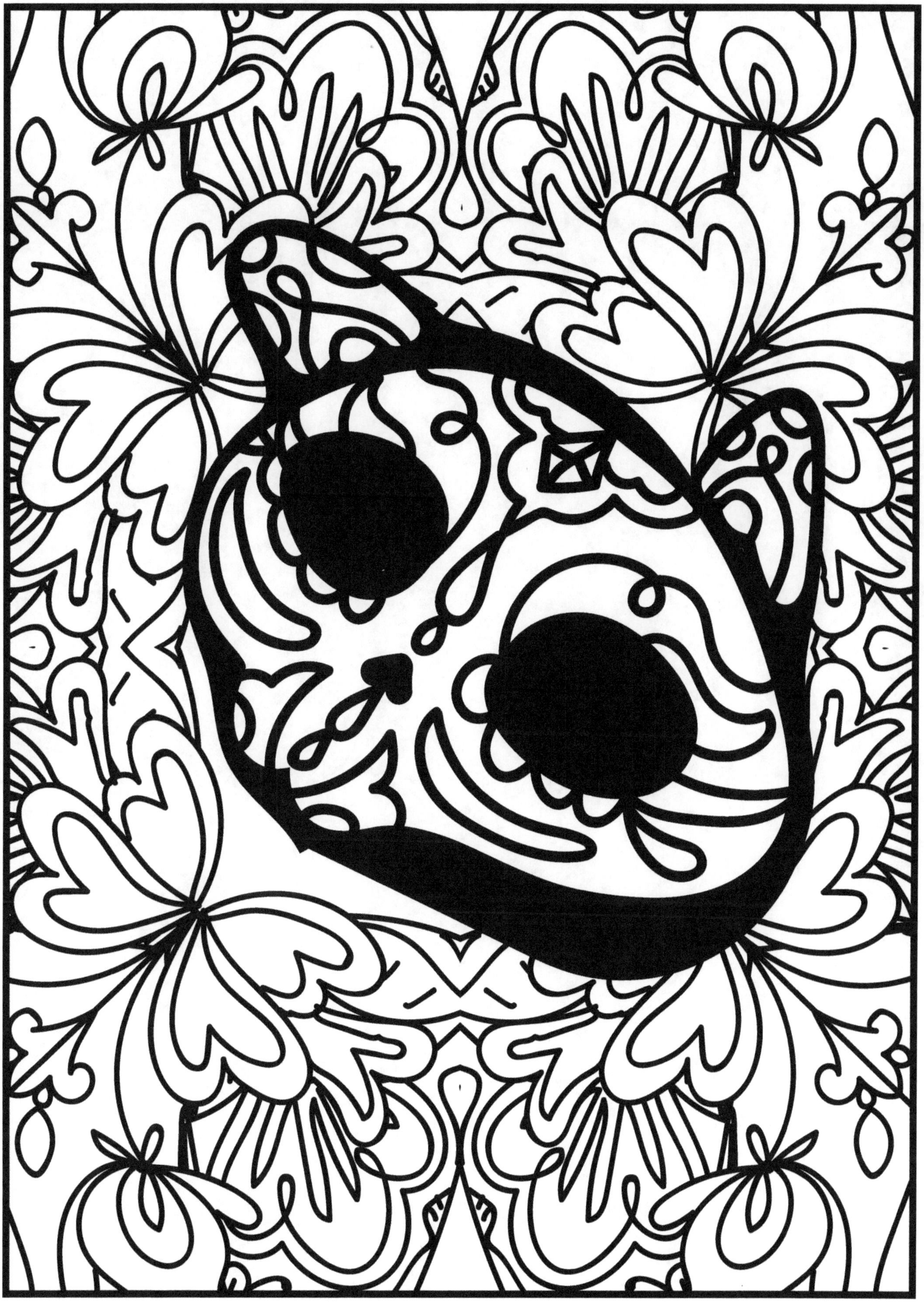

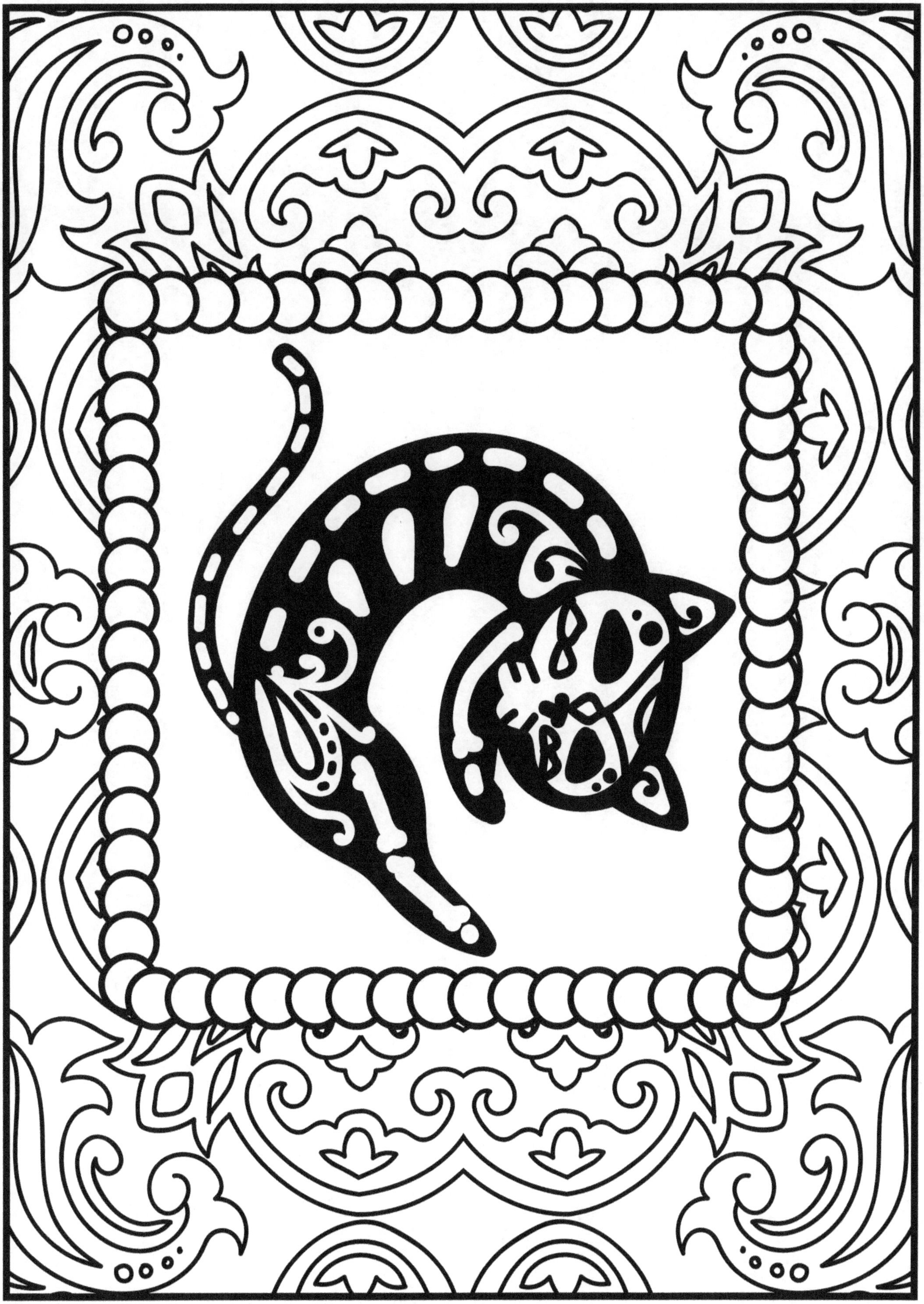

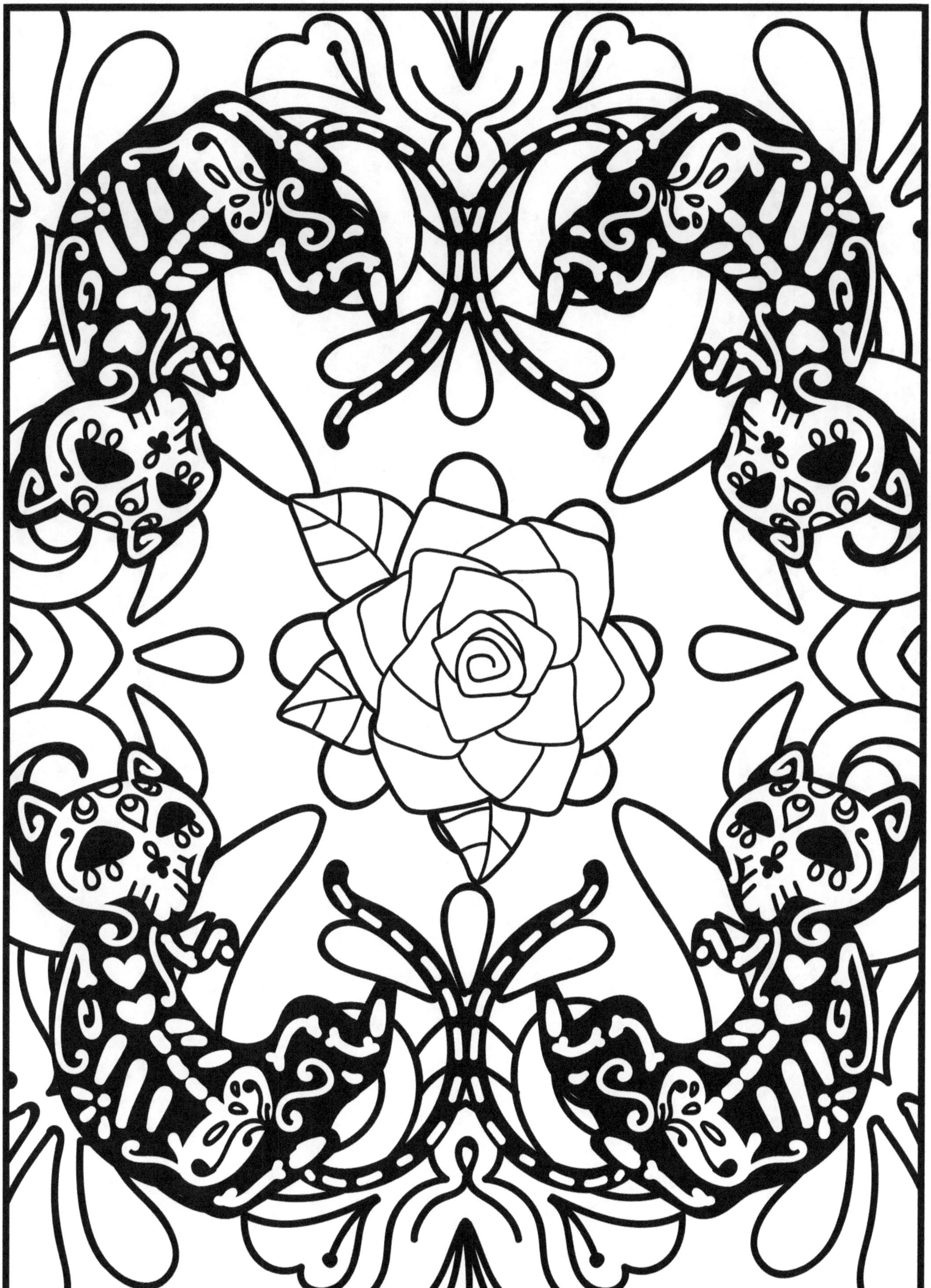

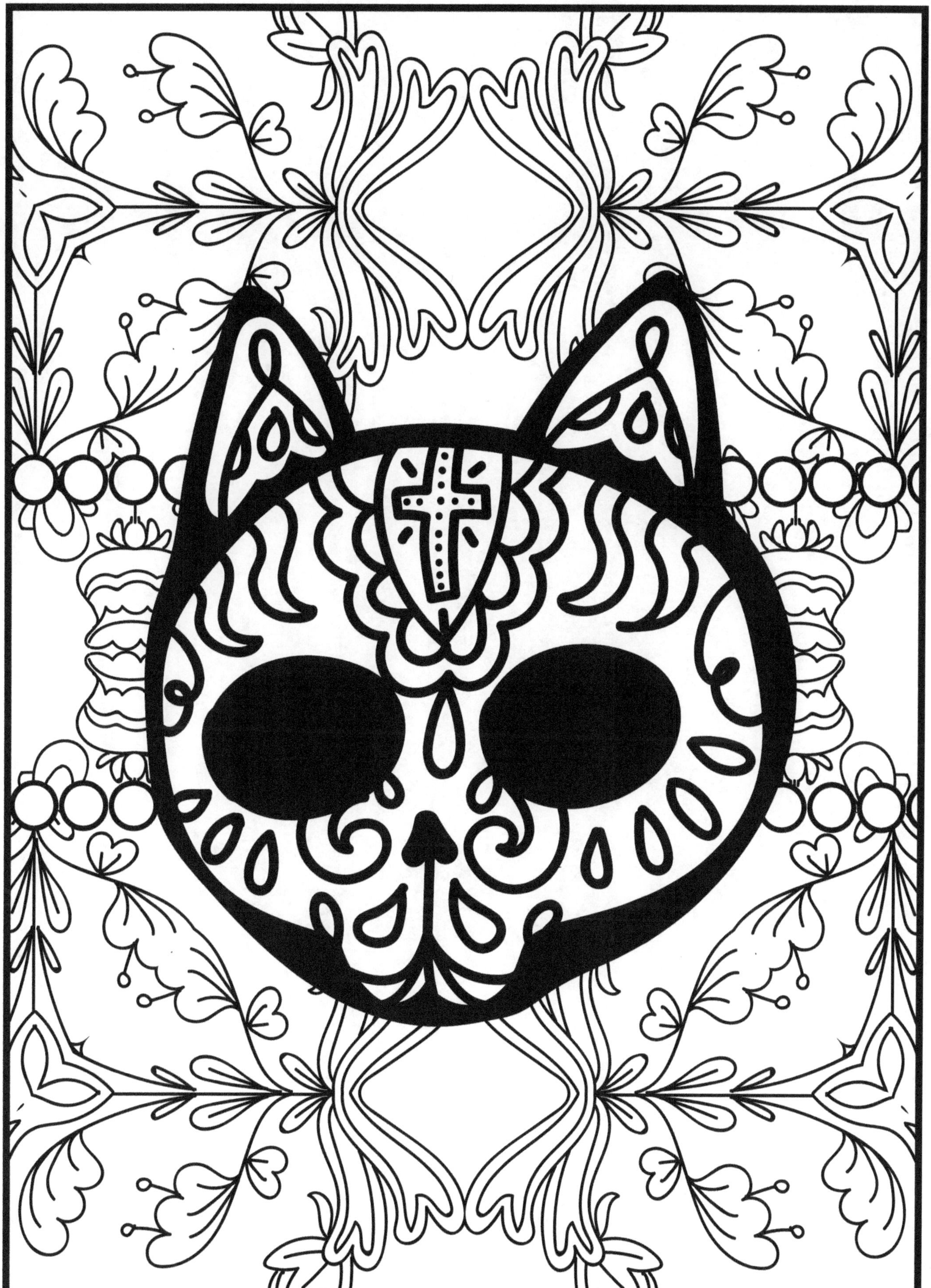

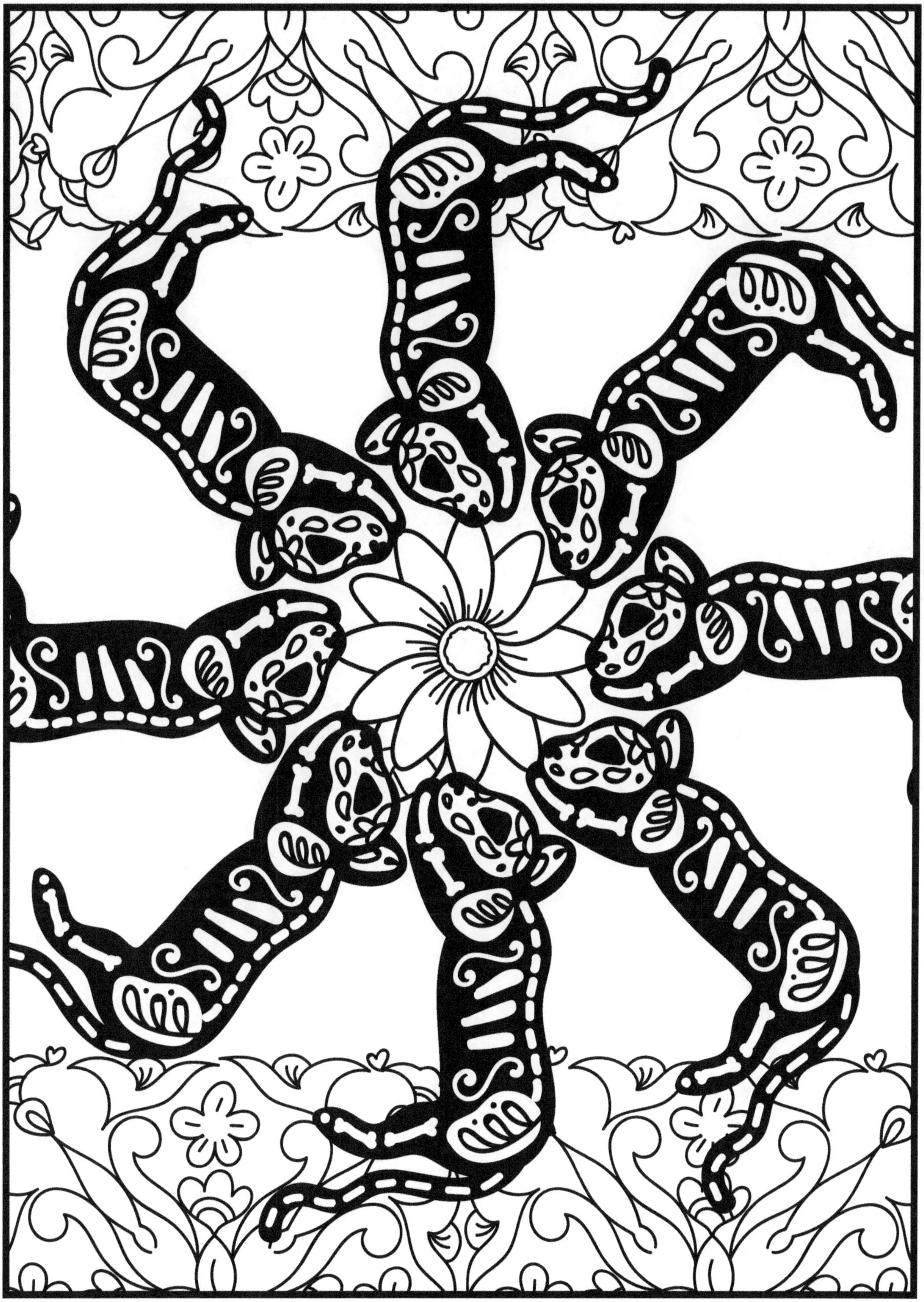

www.ingramcontent.com/pod-product-compliance
Lightning Source LLC
Chambersburg PA
CBHW080622190526
45169CB00009B/3260
* 9 7 8 1 5 3 4 9 4 1 3 6 6 *